THE HONEY

CONNOISSEUR

HONEY

Selecting, Tasting, and **Pairing** Honey, With a Guide to More than **30** Varietals

CONNOISSEUR

C. Marina Marchese **&** Kim Flottum

ILLUSTRATIONS BY Elara Tanguy

BLACK DOG
& LEVENTHAL
PUBLISHERS
NEW YORK

Published by
Black Dog & Leventhal Publishers, Inc.
151 West 19th Street
New York, NY 10011

Distributed by
Workman Publishing Company
225 Varick Street
New York, NY 10014

Manufactured in Singapore

Cover and interior design by Red Herring Design

Cover photograph by Andrew Purcell

ISBN-13: 978-1-57912-929-3

h g f e d c b a

Library of Congress Cataloging-in-Publication Data available on file.

DEDICATION

FROM KIM...

Marina certainly is the inspiration for this work. We have
worked together on projects in the past and this was the
next step for each of us. Her focus is on the magic of how
and why honey comes to be. Mine shows where and when
honey is born. Each of us following a passion has produced
what you now read. Passions, though, are fueled by many
fires. My other passion, my best friend and my greatest
source of support and balance, Kathy, made this book,
and everything, possible. Thanks Kath.

FROM MARINA...

Without Kim, this book would not be complete.
Without Vic, there would not be time to write it.
Without Becky, no one would ever read it.
Without the bees, there would be no honey.
Without beekeepers, there would be no passion.
Without honey lovers, there would be no reason.
A heart-full of thanks to all those who came on the
journey and have embraced this sweet work.

CONTENTS

CHAPTER 1

LA DOLCE VITA

In the Valley of the Kings on the West Bank at Luxor there is a tomb named KV 62 that was cut during Egypt's eighteenth dynasty. It belongs to the Egyptian pharaoh Tutankhamen. Discovered in 1922 by Howard Carter, it is considered one of the most significant archaeological discoveries of the twentieth century. As was the tradition in ancient Egypt, the pharaoh was buried with a cache of artifacts, including furniture, garments, and food. Among these articles were clay vessels filled with olive oil and wine.

The vessels were inscribed with detailed notes naming the type of wine, the producer, the geographic region in which it was produced, and the date when the jar was sealed. Nearby were two more vessels described by Carter as drab pottery with double handles, bound with rush and secured with clay seals. The shoulders of these vessels carried the identification of the contents, written from right to left, in black hieratic script, depicting the word for honey bee. When the clay seals were removed, the insides of the jars revealed honey, completely preserved, still almost liquid, and retaining its original sweet aroma. These offerings of honey, olive oil, and wine were placed in King Tut's tomb alongside his body because it was believed that he would need these items in his afterlife. More than three thousand years later, the olive oil and wine had spoiled, but the honey remained intact and edible.

Bees and honey played an important part in the everyday life of the Egyptians. They were the first nomadic beekeepers, floating their hives up and down the Nile following the seasonal blooms. Their main sources for nectar were orange, clover, and cotton. Honey was removed from the hives by smoking out the bees, then crushing the comb and straining the honey into clay jars. It was used as a culinary sweetener, as well as for mead and medicine. Ancient medical texts written on papyrus describe honey as being used for ointments and touting its therapeutic effects on wounds. The walls of tombs were rich in bee imagery depicting scenes of beekeeping and honey production. Cleopatra, the last ruling pharaoh, celebrated for her beauty, was said to be indebted to honey inside and out. After her ritual of bathing in milk and honey she indulged in her favorite snack, a sweet honey nut truffle called *dulcis coccora*.

Honey, like wine and olive oil, was considered a luxury by the Egyptians and was stored in clay amphorae or wooden flat-bottom vessels. The chards recovered from Tutankhamen's tomb revealed that each amphora was carefully labeled with information including the honey's source or provenance, the date and location of its production, and the name of the person who sealed the jar. The origin and quality of agricultural products obviously played an important role in ancient societies. The title "sealer of the honey" was given to those respected people who oversaw the act of sealing the honey-filled vessels, ensuring quality control. The descriptions of these practices are the earliest references to *terroir* and the high value placed on agricultural commodities.

The Science and Art of Making Honey

Honey is made by honey bees from the nectar of flowers. Inside every beehive is a honey-making factory buzzing with activity where nature's virtu-ose are transforming the floral nectar into the sweetest elixir on the planet. A worker honey bee will make just $\frac{1}{12}$ teaspoon of this culinary masterpiece in her short life. Hundreds of varieties of honey are harvested here in the United States, and thousands around the world. Many are limited harvests, produced seasonally and remaining local to their region. The recipe never changes, only the flower, the nectar, the season, and the region in which it's collected. It's these factors that make every jar of honey unique in color, aroma, and flavor.

Honey is exclusively the creation of the female worker honey bees, who are also responsible for almost all other hive duties, including brood rearing, collecting nectar and pollen, cleaning house, building beeswax comb, defending the hive, and attending to the queen. The queen will outlive all of her daughters and sons because of her special diet of royal jelly, but she does not directly contribute to honey production in any way. The colony is also made up of a smaller, seasonal population of male bees called drones, whose main purpose is to mate with a queen from another colony, but they also serve other purposes. When drones are present the hive's population is in balance. Drones act as heat sinks aiding the colony by giving off heat from their warm bodies on cool spring and summer evenings. They also produce a series of pheromones that help motivate workers to collect both nectar and pollen.

Worker bees begin foraging for water, pollen, nectar, and propolis (a resinous material used to repair and maintain the hive) when they're about twenty-one days old. The honey-making process begins in a sunny field of blooming flowers, where a worker bee chooses to visit the most attractive flowers with the sweetest-smelling nectar. She hovers over its petals, then gracefully lands, probing the flower to locate the nectar, and begins sipping up the nectar with her long, tube-like tongue called a proboscis. When she is satisfied, she seeks out more flowers of the same species until her nectar-carrying storage container, called a honey sac, is full. Then she carries her bounty back to her hive. A worker bee's tiny body is capable of carrying more than her own weight in nectar. While the bee is on the way home, the nectar is mixed inside the honey sac with an enzyme called invertase, beginning the transformation into honey. Once back at the hive she transfers her load to her sisters to continue the honey-making process.

A worker bee inside the hive accepts the nectar from the foraging bee and manipulates it with her mouthparts for a time, exposing it to the hive's dry air, and adding even more enzymes. She then hangs it on the top of one of the hexagonal beeswax cells that make up the entire honey bee nest. After the nectar is placed in a cell, the bees set to work reducing its water content by fanning their wings to produce a continuous breeze, a process aided by the high temperature in the hive. This action dries and ripens the nectar, which, when it is dehydrated to about 17–18 percent moisture, becomes thick, sweet, pure honey. The bees consolidate the resulting honey from many partially filled cells to fewer cells that are full of honey. They then cover or cap each honey-filled cell with beeswax to keep it safe and fresh. Honey remains pristine inside these cells until it is needed by the bees to sustain the colony. Given sufficient space inside a hive and compatible weather conditions, a healthy, strong colony of honey bees will continually produce and store honey as long as nectar is available and they are able to collect it. The bees need some of this bounty for their daily food, and seek to store enough to see them through the winter. Any excess honey is what the beekeeper will harvest.

The Harvest

The best part of beekeeping is the sweet reward of the honey harvest, which comes both during and at the end of a prosperous season, depending on the floral sources of

Scout Bees

Scout bees are specially designated worker bees that seek out the flowers by returning to familiar locations and searching for attractive scents for other foraging honey bees. Once a location is found that has a lot of flowers, each with nectar and high sugar content, the scout bee returns to the hive to communicate her findings to other foragers through a series of highly sophisticated dances that show the flowers' location in relationship to the hive and the sun. She also shares the taste and aroma of the new flowers. After observing the dances and smelling and tasting a sample of the nectar, the other worker bees will determine if the source of nectar is attractive. If so they will set out from the hive to find that source of the nectar. If not, they wait for a scout with a better find. In any event, once the chosen source of nectar is found the worker bee uses the colors and designs on a flower's petals, called nectar guides, in order to locate the nectary deep within each flower.

a specific region. When winemakers are harvesting their grapes and olives are being pressed into oil, beekeepers are extracting honey from the combs. Once the surplus honey has been completely cured and capped over by the bees, it is ready to be removed from the hive.

Inside each honey super, or wooden box, that makes up a modern beehive are multiple wooden frames. As bees make the honey, they fill the thousands of cells of beeswax honeycomb on each frame. When the frames are bursting with honey, the bee-keeper's work begins. To extract the honey from the beeswax, the beekeeper must first coax the bees away from the frames. There are several ways to accomplish this. One way is to gently guide the bees off the honey frames using a tool called a bee escape, which allows the bees from the top box of the hive to exit and go to the lower box by way of a one-way door. Once below, they can't return. A second way is to apply an aromatic substance on a fume board, which sends the bees away from the frames to another part of the hive. Once the bees are moved away from the honey, the beekeeper can remove the boxes, or supers, that contain the frames and bring them to the honey house, where honey extraction can begin.

The first step in extraction is to bring the supers and their contents to room tempera-ture so the wax will be soft and the honey will flow easily. Once warm each frame is removed from the boxes and the beekeeper, using a large, sharp knife carefully removes the beeswax covering from the honey-filled cells. The process is called uncapping and is usually accomplished using an uncapping knife, which can be room temperature or warmed slightly. Uncapping frames is done over a deep tray called an uncapping tank; as the cells are uncapped, the wax cappings fall into the tank below. The uncapped frames are then placed in racks inside a round stainless-steel tank called an extractor, which spins the racks and frames, using

centrifugal force to spin the honey out of the beeswax cells, much like a lettuce spinner. As the honey is pulled from the cells by the spinning extractor, it hits the sides of the tank and runs to the bottom of the barrel, where it can easily be drawn from a gate at the bottom. When all the honey has been removed from the frames, the beekeeper opens the gate to access the honey. Honey runs out of the gate and usually passes through a course strainer to be collected in a container. The strainer catches any random wax particles, stray bees, or debris from the hive. The container is commonly a five-gallon plastic pail that has a sealable lid to keep the honey clean and safe. The pail is left to sit for several days, and any remaining pieces of wax, errant bees, air bubbles, or other material will rise to the surface. The beekeeper will skim this off, leaving clean, clear honey that is ready to be poured into bottles, labeled, and taken to market. This is the beekeeper's reward.

Pollination

Honey bees not only make honey, but in the process of gathering nectar and pollen, they also pollinate many of our fruits, vegetables, seeds, nuts, spices, herbs, and ornamental flowers. Farmers rely on honey bees to pollinate plants like protein-rich clover and alfalfa to feed their livestock. Well-fed animals make our meats, eggs, cheeses, and milk tastier. Even the plants that provide the necessary fats and oils in our diet require honey bee pollination. Other popular crops that require pollination include coffee, choc-olate, and cotton. A world without honey bees would mean a world without many of the foods and products we need every day.

Pollination begins when the tiny grains of pollen produced by the anther, the male reproductive part of the flower, are moved to the female part, called the stigma. Once on the stigma's surface, the pollen produces

a tube that grows down the style to reach the ovary, where fertilization occurs and the plant produces a seed. Once fertilization has occurred, a fruit begins to grow around the developing seeds. Pollinators such as birds, bats, butterflies, bees, and even the wind move pollen between plants. All benefit in the economy of nature; flowering plants are able to produce seeds, and pollinators are given nectar and pollen to meet their energy requirements to produce offspring.

Honey bees visit many flowers on a foraging excursion. Their hairy bodies naturally collect pollen while they move from flower to flower seeking nectar. A foraging bee will revisit the same kind of flower repeatedly on a single foraging excursion, a unique behavior called flower fidelity. If she prefers clover, she will be loyal to clover, moving pollen from clover blossom to clover blossom. This is how a pure, varietal honey is produced.

It is often easy to tell whether a flower has been pollinated. Fully pollinated cucumbers, for example, are straight and fully developed from end to end, not skinny on one end; melons and squash are firm, heavy and juicy, while each drupelet of a raspberry is plump. Apples that are properly pollinated are round and full. The seeds of a watermelon tell us a lot about pollination. The black seeds are pollinated, and the white seeds are not. The more black seeds, the sweeter and larger the watermelon. It takes pollinated seeds to produce the hormones that cause fruits and vegetables to grow, ripen and develop good flavor. Fruits or vegetables not fully pollinated are often lopsided and curl or twist into unusual shapes.

The Composition of Honey

The composition of honey varies depending on the source of the nectar and the type of soil, climate, wind, and sun that the plant is exposed to during a season. Of course, how well the honey is harvested and stored also has an effect on honey composition. Generally speaking, honey is a complex carbohydrate composed of approximately 80 percent monosaccharides, or simple sugars, mostly fructose (levulose) and glucose (dextrose) in varying ratios depending on the nectar source. The remaining content, approximately 16–18 percent, is water. Fructose is slightly sweeter than glucose and, when it occurs in larger quantities than the glucose, can lead to rapid crystallization of the honey. Over twenty-five other disaccharides have been identified in honey —sucrose, maltose, maltulose, kojibiose, and turanose among them—and also present are oligosaccharides, including erlose, theanderose, and panos. These are not naturally present in nectar but are formed during the honey ripening process.

One of the most important attributes of any honey is its water content. The average water content of most good-quality honeys is 17–18 percent, because bees make it that way, though there are a few exceptions. Yeast is also present in all honeys as a result of being in the environment in general, on plants, and in the hive. When water and yeast combine in honey, the honey remains stable because, even though the yeast can use the sugars in the honey as fuel, it needs more water to flourish. Honey is hygroscopic and when the water content is higher than 18 percent, the naturally occurring yeast begins to grow, using the water and the sugars in the honey, and thus beginning the process of fermentation.

Proteins make up about twenty-five percent of honey composition and there are at least 19 different ones present. The proteins are mainly enzymes added by the bees during the ripening process. Invertase, the most significant enzyme, is what sets honey apart from other sweeteners. This important enzyme enables the fundamental conversion of the large-molecule sugar sucrose, commonly found in nectar, to divide into the two smaller sugars that turn nectar into honey: glucose and fructose. Enzymes also add nutritional value and are highly sensitive to heat. Honey contains a few amino acids and the most important is proline, some of which is derived from the plant source and some added by the bees. Proline is the measure of honeys ripeness and is important standard for judging quality and flavor profile.

Most honeys are rather acid with a pH value that can range from 3.4 to 6.0. On average it is 3.9 and acidity increases with fermentation, but the acidity is camouflaged by its sweetness. Gluconic acid is the most prominent acid found in honey and it adds flavor-enhancing properties. It occurs when bees add their glucose oxidase to nectar during the ripening process to stabilize the ripening nectar against spoilage. It is also responsible for transforming the glucose into gluconic acid and hydrogen peroxide (H_2O_2) imparting the anti-bacterial properties in honey. The anti-bacterial properties of glucose oxidase are most active when when eaten or when diluted in water.

Honey contains a wide variety of minerals including potassium and trace elements. In general, darker honeys that are stronger in flavor have a higher mineral content. These elements make it possible to identify different types of varietal honeys.

Honey also contains over six hundred volatile organic compounds (VOC) or plant-based essential oils, many originate from the plant and some are added by the bee. Each compound represents a detailed profile or fingerprint of any specific honey providing us with valuable information concerning the honey's botanical and

geographical origin. These VOC's contribute to the sensory characteristics and act as floral origin markers giving every harvest of honey its unique aroma and flavor profile. Volatile organic compounds evaporate from honey when the honey is heated and this is why heating honey compromises its delicate flavors.

Honey can easily spoil without proper care and storage. Hydroxymethylfurfural (HMF) is naturally present in all honeys and is a product of the decomposition of fructose. Its concentration increases in honeys that have been treated with heat or stored for extended periods of time at elevated temperatures. The HMF content is used as a standard criterion to measure freshness and its presence is an indication of honey that has been overheated. The higher the HMF number, the lower the quality of the honey.

Kinds of Honey

Honey is found in different forms depending on how it is harvested or prepared by the beekeeper, its water and sugar content, and even the local conditions.

COMB HONEY

Comb honey is liquid honey that has not been extracted and is still inside the original beeswax cells, exactly how the bees made it. Whether it is inside a hive managed by a beekeeper or inside a tree produced by wild honey bees, honeycomb could be considered virgin honey, untouched by humans. When the fragile beeswax comb is sliced or spread, the fresh liquid honey oozes out of the cells. The flavor is extremely delicate, and the waxy texture contrasts nicely on the palate with the smooth honey, providing a textural experience of smooth and chewy all in one bite.

Honey still in the beeswax comb can be obtained in several forms. The most natural is when the beekeeper provides the bees with a small round plastic or sometimes square basswood frame, called a section, for the bees to directly build their honeycomb in. These are generally about a quarter of the size of one of the wooden frames in which bees normally build their comb. When the comb is completely filled with honey and capped, it is harvested, covered with a protective wrap, and sold directly, container and all, to the consumer. This is comb honey at it purest, totally untouched by human hands.

Cut comb honey is a bit different. In that case, an entire frame is harvested, and, because it is large, the beekeeper cuts it into smaller pieces, about the same size as section comb honey described above, lets the honey from the cut frame edge drain overnight, then puts it in a protective package to sell.

And finally, there's chunk honey, a mix of comb honey and liquid honey. Cut comb honey pieces are made small enough to fit into glass jars. Sometimes two, three, or more are cut, puzzle-like, to fit in a jar. Creative beekeepers may combine different types of comb honey, including a very dark honey, a medium honey, and a very light honey, in the same jar. The empty space in the jar is then filled with liquid honey, surrounding the chunks and adding an interesting visual dimension to a honey product.

Honeycomb is a special treat that should be experienced by everyone. Spread honeycomb on a slice of toasted bread alone or with butter. Or pair it with a handcrafted cheese, preferably a triple cream, and your favorite bread or cracker. It is not advisable to put honeycomb into hot tea unless you do not mind the tiny chunks of wax that float to the top or stick to the sides of your teacup. Since honeycomb is taken directly from the hive and handled minimally by the beekeeper, it is said to have more health benefits than most liquid types of honey. When selecting honeycomb, look for pearly white wax filled, preferably, with a lightly colored, golden honey. The wax cappings should be even and consistently smooth without stains or leaky punctures.

LIQUID HONEY

Liquid honey, also called extracted honey, is honey that has been separated or extracted from the wax honeycomb. There are many different techniques to extract liquid honey, and some are less invasive to its fragile properties than others. Once liquid honey has been harvested and separated from its original wax, its sensory qualities change depending on the technique used by the beekeeper. Liquid honey is the most versatile type of honey. It can be mixed easily into recipes or drizzled to pair with food or finish a dish.

CRYSTALLIZED HONEY

Liquid honey is a supersaturated sugar solution waiting to return to solid form. It does that when sugar molecules come out of the sugar-water solution and form sugar crystals by joining together and leaving the water behind. This crystallization begins with one sugar crystal adhering to a microscopic speck in the honey such as another sugar crystal, a piece of dust, or a pollen grain. Once that occurs, other sugar molecules have a substrate to adhere to, and they too can come out of solution. The crystal that is formed depends on the temperature of the honey, the size of the original crystal, and the ratio of glucose to fructose in the honey. Sometimes the crystals are large and grainy, both unattractive and unpalatable. But if the honey is "seeded" with tiny, fine crystals that are well dispersed in the jar, the finished product, a crystallized honey made of small, fine crystals, is delectable and the mouth feel is smooth, almost buttery.

The Products of the Hive

Besides honey, honey bees make other products of value not only to themselves but also useful to beekeepers. Beeswax, bee-collected pollen, propolis, royal jelly, and bee venom have been used for health and healing for centuries. Apitherapy, the science of using products from the hive (api means "bee"), is practiced around the world using these five products produced by honey bees.

BEESWAX

Beeswax is secreted from special glands on the underside of a worker bee's abdomen. Neither drones nor queens can make beeswax. After harvesting honey, beekeepers save the beeswax cappings, chunks of wax from errant comb the bees produce in stray places in the hive, from comb that's

been broken or damaged and is therefore unusable by the bees, or from comb that has grown old and dark. A colony of honey bees will need to produce and then consume several pounds of honey in order to create enough beeswax to fill the frames of the hive with honeycomb, so from a bee's perspective it is a labor-intensive project. Harvesting and cleaning beeswax are also labor-intensive activities for the beekeeper, but beeswax has all sorts of uses, as elegant candles, healing balms and salves, and is pressed into sheets that are used as foundation inside the wooden frames for bees to begin building honeycomb on. Beeswax is used to wax skis, boats, and knitting needles.

NECTAR AND POLLEN

Honey bees gather both nectar and pollen from flowers during their foraging trips. Sometimes it's just nectar; sometimes, when there is a large brood population waiting back home that needs a high-protein diet, the foragers collect only pollen; and sometimes it's both. On the way back to the hive, the bees move any pollen sticking to their hairy bodies to special hairs on their back legs and in the process add a bit of nectar and sugar to the powdery pollen, along with special enzymes. The nectar makes the pollen easier to pack and when mixed with those enzymes allows the pollen to ferment,

Honeydew

Honeydew is the sugary liquid waste secreted by aphids or scale insects after feeding on sap from some conifer or other trees. Honey bees will gather this liquid and carry it back to the hive and make honey from it. Also referred to as manna, honeydew is highly prized and in other countries is commonly consumed in culinary recipes and even as a medicine. Typically, honeydew honeys have lower amounts of fructose and glucose and higher amounts of complex sugars. Honeydew does not normally crystallize or contain pollen, nor is it considered blossom honey in the truest sense. It is usually very dark and high in dextrin and minerals. It is referred to by and marketed as the species of tree it is produced from and often called fir, oak, pine, beech, or spruce forest honey.

so that it can be stored for later use. Pollens vary from flower to flower in the amount of proteins they have, as well as the kinds of minerals and vitamins and even some enzymes they carry, so a colony of bees needs pollen from a wide variety of plants in order to maintain a balanced and nutritious diet.

In order to harvest some of the pollen that the bees have collected, beekeepers place special grids at the entrance to the hive that the bees must pass through, knocking off some of the pollen off their back legs that they bring back to the hive. The pollen is collected in a box below the hive and the beekeeper harvests it from there. Beekeepers sell this harvested pollen as a dietary supplement for humans or to save and feed back to hungry hives later in the season.

PROPOLIS

Propolis is a resinous substance that bees use to seal small cracks and crevices in their hives so pests and diseases can't enter, to fasten hive boxes together, to give strength to fragile beeswax cells, to smooth rough interior boards, and even to seal large openings, like the front door if they feel it's too large. Beekeepers call propolis "bee glue." Propolis also has antibacterial and antifungal properties and is being studied for other medicinal properties. It is commonly used to treat a wide range of illnesses—minor cuts and scrapes, burns and abrasions for instance— and is sometimes found in natural mouthwashes, toothpastes, and throat lozenges.

To make propolis, bees first gather plant resins, mostly from the developing leaves and flower buds of certain trees in the spring and summer. Resin is secreted by the trees to protect the buds from insects and diseases while the buds are in their juvenile stage. The bees then add several enzymes to the resin, along with a bit of beeswax. Different trees produce different resins, so not all propolis is created equal. Beekeepers collect odd bits and pieces of propolis from

woodenware inside the hive or harvest it more systematically by planting grids with tiny slits in the hive that the bees fill with propolis and the beekeeper can then remove by scraping it away. Propolis can be rolled into sticky balls and sucked on as a lozenge or mixed with grain alcohol as a tincture.

ROYAL JELLY

Royal jelly is a food produced in glands near the mouthparts of worker bees that are only a couple of weeks old. It is composed of sugar, protein, and a variety of enzymes, vitamins, and minerals. It is the best food there is for a honey bee, so all bees—workers, drones, and especially queens—are fed this special diet by these two-week-old workers for the first three days or so of life. The diets of workers and drones change to pollen and honey as they mature and develop, but queens continue to receive royal jelly all their life, and as a result develop into large, healthy, sexually complete females, rather than their less developed worker bee sisters.

Beekeepers can harvest royal jelly, with a great degree of difficulty, because there is very little of it to be found, and sell it for use by humans as health supplements or as additives to cosmetics. It can be mixed with honey and sometimes with pollen, but it is an extremely bitter, foul-tasting liquid to eat by itself. It's a wonder bees eat it at all.

BEE VENOM

The most surprisingly beneficial product of honey bees is bee venom. People who suffer from ailments that traditional medicine has not been able to cure turn to the sting from a honey bee for relief. Bee venom therapy is similar to acupuncture in that micro-stings are given to patients along the same meridians in order to allow energy to flow. Bee venom therapy is used around the world to treat lyme disease, multiple sclerosis and rheumatoid arthritis.

CHAPTER }2

TERROIR:
A PORTRAIT OF THE LAND

If you have noticed that local blueberries at your farmer's market are delicious, plentiful, and affordably priced in midsummer, then you are acquainted with terroir. If you appreciate that the meal you prepared from what you grew in your own garden tastes better than the one you ate at a restaurant, then you have fully experienced terroir.

More challenging to pronounce than it is to understand, terroir is the French word for "earth"— not dirt, but soil and a host of environmental factors, notably the location of the soil. It is the reason those blueberries grew well there, that they enjoyed a soil that is well drained with a low pH and a climate with cooler winters. If they are plump and juicy, thank the terroir and the bees that pollinated them.

Goût de terroir or "taste of earth" is the centuries-old French concept that declares that wines produced in certain legally defined areas, called appellations, express those particular regions in taste and flavor. It also maintains that these wines cannot be duplicated in any other region without noticeable differences to its sensory qualities. This legal regulation is exercised in the form of a certification, called *Appellation d'origine contrôlée* (AOC), or Controlled Designations of Origin, which protects and identifies wine-producing regions. It is also granted to cheese, honey, and other agricultural products that express their native terrain. The French, like many other producers around the world, are extremely proud of their terroir and take it very seriously. Some winemakers have gone as far as to taste their soil

before planting their grapes, to ensure the best flavor characteristics for their harvest.

Terroir has been associated with wine for centuries, and winemakers understand the terroir of the region in which they grow their grapes and how it affects their wine. But recently terroir has also been attributed to the sensory qualities of tea, coffee, chocolate, and honey. Terroir is the story of the plants, animals, soil, geography, and climate of a place. It's the unique mark Mother Nature leaves on the color, aroma, and flavor of all agricultural products produced in a clearly defined area. It is why the unusually sweet Vidalia onion grows only in Georgia, and why Wisconsin's loamy soil is host to luscious grasses that dairy cows forage on to produce their tongue-twanging cheddar cheese. It's the reason mesquite flourishes in the deserts of Arizona and that its honey has the aroma and flavor of warm sand.

Terroir is now being applied by beekeepers to the honey they produce, although the concept is even more complex with respect to honey than to wine. Honey produced from the same type of plant will have slightly different sensory characteristics when produced in two different regions. Clover honey produced in the midwestern United States is lighter in color and grassier in flavor than clover honey produced on the East Coast. Soil, climate, water, wind, and sun all contribute to every honey's sensory attributes, including color, aroma, and flavor. That unpredictable mosaic of natural conditions ensures the subtle, but ever-changing profile of a varietal honey.

Region is not the only determinant, however. A honey bee colony that forages in the same field of clover could yield a honey that is remarkably different in color, aroma, and flavor from one year to the next. This is often because other types of plants besides clover bloom in that field at the same time the clover blooms, and honey bees mix the different nectars together inside the hive, creating an unpredictable

flavor profile for every honey harvest.

It is also true in the theme of terroir that honey harvests can be extremely productive, average, or terrible in any given year. Mother Nature always has the last word. It is terroir that dictates which honey harvest will be bountiful and which flavors will be distinct and bright. These variables in honey production can and do change from year to year due to the ever-changing variables of the region that contributes to the final product. Often it seems that some of the best honeys are produced by chance—a quirk of rainfall, an unexpected heat wave, a cold snap that arrived too early, or even something as simple as a sea breeze.

Such unpredictable combinations of agricultural elements are responsible not only for the infinite colors, aromas, and flavor profiles of any honey but also for the quantity and quality of nectar produced. Artisan honeys, those honeys produced by small-scale beekeepers, are particularly vulnerable because they strive to highlight quality and character rather than quantity and consistency. The best honey that a region can offer depends on the local terroir, the characteristics of that location, but also on the beekeeping skills necessary to produce it.

Traditionally, honeys in the United States are named for the flower or plant type from which the nectar is gathered, not after the region where the honey is produced. This is unfortunate, because it neglects the subtle effects of terroir. Labeling all orange blossom honeys as such, no matter where they are produced, offers no details as to what you might expect to find in the color, aroma or flavor of a particular orange blossom honey. If a jar of honey carried on its label the name of the region where it was produced, consumers might have more insight into the effects of terroir and the characteristics of a honey as a product of a particular place. Consumers would have the option to choose their honey not only by plant source, but also by location of origin.

Soil

Terroir begins with the soil. Soil is the complex mineral and organic layer that covers our planet, and it varies considerably by region. The quality of the soil is an indicator of the health of a particular area. It also determines the type of honey plants that are capable of flourishing in a particular region. The largest part of all soil is made up of minerals—fragments of many different types of weathered rocks, as well as living and decaying organisms, including plants and animals. Minerals are an essential part of any soil; when dissolved in rainwater, mixed with air, and absorbed through a plant's roots, they are responsible for the plant's ability to grow, bloom, and yield pollen and nectar. Common minerals that are essential to a plant's health and ability to convert sunlight into energy through photosynthesis include nitrogen, phosphorus, potassium, calcium, and magnesium. The pH of soil—how acidic or alkaline it is—is also a key factor in a plant's ability to prosper and produce nectar. Some honey plants prefer acidic soil and others prefer alkaline. The overall condition of the soil, its quality and fertility, also matters a great deal when it comes to determining not only which type of honey plant will thrive in a particular region but also whether it will survive there.

Soil scientists have classified soil into twelve different orders. All twelve of these soil types are a combination of three general types: very fine particles from eroded rock known as clay; coarser particles from variable rocks like limestone, granite, gypsum, and feldspar, called sand; and loam, which is a combination of clay and sand. Clay soil is practically impermeable and holds less organic matter than either loam or sand. Sandy soil is very porous and has a low mineral content because of its inability to hold the minerals. Loamy soil is rich in with organic matter that retains water and provides necessary nutrients needed for plants. No matter the type of soil, there is a type of honey plant that will thrive in it.

The minerals found in the soil can also give honey its color. Light-colored honeys like citrus, rosemary, lavender, eucalyptus, and thyme contain high amounts of calcium. Darker honeys contain higher amounts of potassium, chlorine, sulfur, sodium, iron, manganese, and magnesium. Iron is what gives buckwheat honey its deep brown color. If iron in the soil becomes oxidized, it gives buckwheat a reddish hue. Glauconitic, or oxided, copper in water-saturated soils can give a green hue to honey like tupelo, while manganese turns up as a purple hue. Hematite adds a rich red tint to soils prevalent in hot desert or tropical climates, which in turn can show up in honey.

What does soil terroir taste like?

Common minerals and rocks found in the soil have significantly distinctive tastes. A few minerals and their taste descriptions follow:

Borax (sweet, alkaline)
Chalcanthite (sweet, metallic, and slightly poisonous)
Epsomite (bitter)
Glauberite (bitter, salty)
Halite (salty)
Hanksite (sulfate; salty)
Melanterite (iron; sweet, astringent, and metallic)
Sylvite (bitter)
Ulexite (alkaline)
Calcium Carbonate (chalky)
Magnesium Silicate (chalky)
Calcium Sulfate (chalky)

Mapping Honey Plants

Botanists and geologists have divided the United States into eight distinct physiographic regions that generally define the distribution of our native flora and vegetation. Each region has its outstanding type of soil, geographic characteristics, and climate that influence the types of honey plants that can be found growing there. We can begin using these regional boundaries as a way of establishing the concept of terroir throughout the United States. Mapping our nation's honey plants is a way to locate where varietal honeys can be produced and why they evolve in very specific conditions. Each of these eight regions has particular seasons, which affect the plants that grow there and their honey or nectar flows.

These distinctive regions can be referred to as American Apicultural Areas (AAA), much like the designated appellations for growing wine grapes in the United States, called American Viticulture Areas (AVA). Beekeepers looking for favorable locations for their bees to forage or looking to produce specific single varietal honeys will find the following list of these regions valuable:

NEW ENGLAND

Thᵢs region is composed of the Northeast and the Adirondack Mountains of northern New York and is defined by sandy, clay loam and limestone soils that are neutral or acidic. The area is defined by forests of pine, spruce, hemlock, maple, birch, and oak and rolling hills and mountains dotted with lakes, swamps, and sandy jagged coastline. The climate is humid, with wet and cloudy springs, warm summers, and cold winters. There are commonly fields of white and alsike clover and all types of berries, including raspberries, blueberries, and huckleberries. Goldenrod and sumac also thrive there

THE APPALACHIAN HIGHLANDS

This region stretches from the Catskills in New York State to northern Georgia and Alabama and from northern New Jersey to eastern Alabama. The area is principally covered by forests of hardwood trees and is characterized by broad valleys and rugged mountains. Sedimentary and volcanic rocks make up this diverse area, and a multitude of rivers and streams provides drainage. The climate is typically cool to warm and wet most of the year. Broadleaf deciduous and evergreens trees characterize this area. Principal honey plants are sourwood, tulip poplar, sumac, honey locust, basswood, willow, and maples.

THE ATLANTIC AND GULF COAST PLAINS

This region includes the area closest to the coast that stretches from Maine to the Mexican border and Virginia to eastern Texas. It's made up of relatively flat areas, with sandy and swampy regions, and is home to pine barren forest, river valleys, wetlands, and marshes. The climate is subtropical, with humid and hot summers then cool, windy winters. High-acidic swamps are fine places for gallberry, black and white tupelo, and black titi to flourish. This area is home to the Pine Barrens and cotton belt.

THE CENTRAL LOWLANDS OR UPPER MISSISSIPPI VALLEY

This region includes the central lowlands of the Gulf Coast Plains and is characterized by grassland prairies and the Mississippi floodplains. The rich soil is composed of sand and wind-blown silt. Primary honey plants are white and sweet clover, sunflowers, asters, Spanish needles, goldenrod, rudbeckia, and gum plants.

THE GREAT PLAINS

This area is due east of the Rocky Mountains between the Rockies and the Mississippi lowlands from Canada to the Rio Grande. It is a vast barren tableland with canyons, buttes, and rugged mountains creating microclimates of extreme temperatures and high winds. Generally arid and with fine soil, these grassland prairies feature abundant amounts of alfalfa and clover to keep commercial beekeepers in business. There are also sagebrush and greasewood.

THE ROCKY MOUNTAINS

This region consists of parts of Idaho, Montana, Wyoming, Utah, Colorado, and New Mexico. It features rugged mountains with high elevations that include the Continental Divide. Bare vegetation, plateaus, and basins are home to spruce, pine, and hemlock forests. Alfalfa and clover can be found chiefly in Montana and Wyoming.

WEST ROCKY MOUNTAINS

This region includes the desert regions of the Sierra Nevada and from eastern Washington State all the way to the cactus deserts of Texas. The climate is similar to that of the Mediterranean. It is dry with low humidity and frequent thunderstorms. Rolling hills, deep valleys, including Death Valley, and sandy, alkaline flats are characteristic of the area. Sagebrush grows in the north, and in the southern plains there are cactus, yucca, and agave. The mountainous regions are covered with coniferous trees, mesquite, saguaro, and other cacti and alfalfa.

THE PACIFIC COAST

This region includes Alaska, Washington, Oregon, and California along the Pacific Coast. It's characterized by heavy rainfall in the north, as well as ocean breezes, high coastal mountains, low and high deserts and fertile valleys. It is predominately home to fireweed, sage, orange, lavender, and eucalyptus.

Climate and Microclimates

Weather may vary from day to day, but over years or decades it follows a predictable pattern called climate. Climate includes precipitation, cloud cover, air temperature, atmospheric pressure, wind, rain, fog, and humidity; and it has a profound effect on all types of honey plants, as well as the bees that pollinate them and collect their nectar. As the weather follows its seasonal pattern, so do bloom times and nectar flows. In turn, these both affect the quantity and quality of nectar produced by local honey plants. Nectar flow can change depending on the terrain, latitude, altitude, and proximity to bodies of water of each region. When plants grow in their ideal conditions, they naturally produce nectar (assuming they are nectar producers); but when the climate changes, nectar secretion becomes less predictable and potentially less abundant.

Within some larger geographic regions lie smaller areas that defy the normal climate, called microclimates. They are commonly found near bodies of water, urban areas, or hilly regions, where the temperature, rainfall, and general weather conditions can change drastically within short distances. Whether the north side of your valley is cool and rainy or the southern side is hot and sunny with an occasional warm breeze matters a great deal to honey plants. Very slight temperature changes can disrupt nectar production. In extreme heat nectar may dry up, and plants may shut down. The relative surface temperature of the local soil also changes within regional microclimates. The slope of the terrain can affect the amount and length of sunlight plants receive. Nearby bodies of water can also affect humidity, sea or land breezes, and air and soil temperatures.

Water

Water exists as a liquid, solid, or vapor and moves between each of those states continuously within the earth's hydrological cycle. It may begin as hail or snow, then melt into a liquid rain, then finally evaporate into fog or clouds. As water moves between those states, it mirrors the local terroir, reflecting the character of the local atmosphere and soil. Water can deposit minerals or deplete them from the soil and change its composition, texture, and ability to hold or absorb heat. Local conditions can ultimately affect the physical and sensory qualities of water, turning it hard or soft, with a high mineral or acidic content. The minerals found in water give it its characteristic taste.

Honey plants and honey bees need water to survive. But sometimes water can hinder honey bee activity and even nectar secretion or pollen production. A pounding rain can wash away an entire nectar flow while flowers are in bloom. An unexpected late snowstorm can destroy early blooming flowers, as often happens when apple trees bloom very early in the Northeast. And an early snowstorm can end an autumn honey flow from goldenrod and asters.

Wind

Wind can dramatically affect the temperature or humidity of a local region. Cool breezes are known to lower temperatures and cool down areas where extreme heat hinders maximum nectar secretion. Wind can also gently dehydrate nectar, which can be helpful to honey bees if not done to excess. Probably most important, breezes over about fifteen miles per hour will ground foraging honey bees, so even when all other factors are conducive to nectar gathering, if bees can't fly, they can't collect nectar and pollen.

Sun

Plants need energy from sunlight plus carbon dioxide from the atmosphere for photosynthesis to occur. Photosynthesis is the process by which plants convert light into energy to produce sugar and oxygen. The amount of sunlight available to a plant is determined by location, season, and climate and directly influences the process of photosynthesis and ultimately the secretion of nectar. Photosynthesis is so essential to plants that they will change their growing patterns in order to absorb more sunlight. They slowly bend their stems or turn their flowers and leaves to grow away from darkness. You've probably seen houseplants grow toward the window to gather the most sunlight. Plants that are deprived of sunlight will slowly stop producing nectar and eventually die, ultimately decreasing the chance of a decent honey harvest.

Seasons

There's a general rule of thumb that beekeepers follow about what kind of honey is produced during which season, and there's good physiological reasoning behind that rule. Honeys produced in early to mid-spring tend to be lighter in color and milder in flavor than honeys produced in late spring through summer, which in turn tend to be a bit lighter in color and less robust in flavor than honeys produced in late summer and autumn, which tend to be the darkest and most full-bodied.

That general rule of thumb is supported by the kinds and numbers of plants that bloom during the seasons. Plants that bloom earlier in the year—think apple trees—tend to have relatively more flowers and will therefore send a smaller amount of sugars and proteins to sustain each of those flowers. A plant only has so much energy to expend, so if it produces thousands of blos-

soms, each will be smaller and of less value, whereas a plant with fewer blossoms will be able to send more energy to each blossom. A midsummer crop, such as white Dutch clover, has more time in the warmer weather to become established and so can afford to spend a little more energy on sugar and protein production while also competing with other plants that have the same advantage. Later-blooming plants—goldenrod, for example—need to be very attractive so they can entice as many pollinators as possible as fast as possible so they can set seed before killing frosts end their season. Thus, they produce armfuls of pollen to be additionally attractive to pollinators, and their nectars are rich with minerals and nutrients essential to honey bees.

These scenarios are good guidelines, but there are also many exceptions to the rule. For example, some dark, strong honeys, such as buckeye, are produced early in the spring; and some light, mild honeys, such as loosestrife, are produced later in the season. Then, of course, there are honeys such as buckwheat, which is always very dark to black in color, no matter the season or the location.

The timing of the nectar flow of every plant is crucial to beekeepers and the honey-making process. Missing a peak nectar flow means missing out on an opportunity to produce the most honey possible from that plant. Local conditions in each region and the variety of plant determine whether the nectar will be available in the morning or afternoon, for just a few hours or a few days. If weather conditions are severe, plants may not produce nectar at all, or the quality and quantity could be compromised. So the amount and type of honey that can be made depend upon nectar availability and its seasonality.

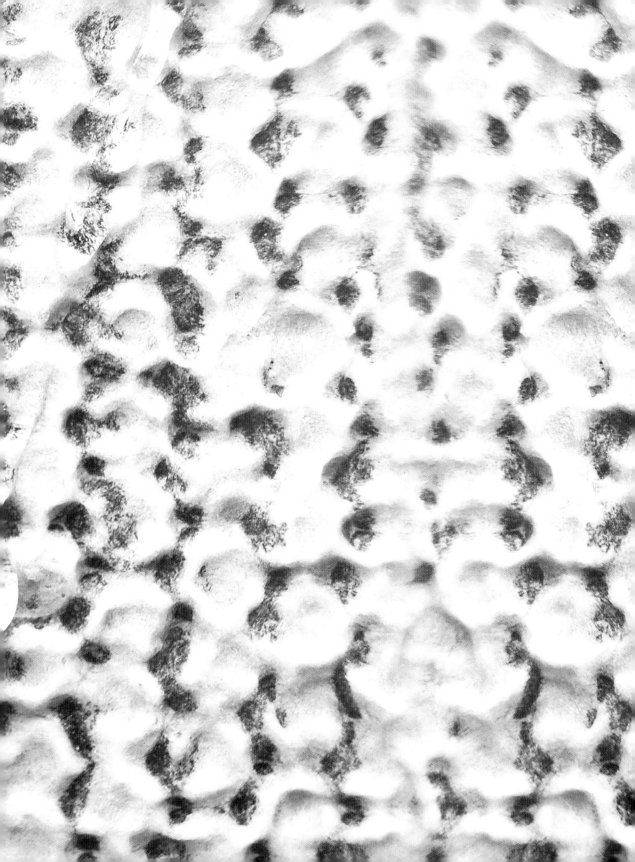

Honey Bee and Beekeeper Activity

Honey bee foraging habits are governed by flower constancy, so if there are large clusters of similar flowers in bloom and the weather cooperates, the chance of a honey harvest is good. Regions closer to the equator generally enjoy longer seasonal bloom periods and diverse vegetation compared to northern areas. Because plants along the equator flourish gradually, the conditions are ideal to produce single-source varietal honeys. Northern areas tend to have less diversity and shorter bloom times, and often bloom periods of different flowers overlap, making it more difficult to produce honey with a single flavor profile. One advantage, however, is that shorter bloom periods contribute to intense nectar flows and larger honey harvests. Honey bees will adapt their foraging habits accordingly but will always seek out the prosperous flowers with the highest sugar content. When a basswood tree is in full bloom and secreting nectar, it will have many flowers continuously blooming, and honey bees have the potential to gather large quantities of nectar over a short period of time or find a more desirable source. Sometimes there is competition from other pollinators that are also seeking nectar during the bloom season. When nectar sources become limited, honey bees may have to work harder and forage farther to gather what they need to make honey to survive. Every jar of honey is a detailed profile of which honey plants were blooming in a particular region at a very specific moment in time.

Indeed, it is the activity of the honey bee that makes the terroir of honey more complex than that of any other agricultural product, including wine and olive oil. We can't ignore that the bees are an integral part of the honey-making process. Honey bees work in harmony with nature, and it is as essential for beekeepers to understand their bees' activities as it is for them to know the soil, climate, and terrain in which the bees forage.

Honey bees are also subject to pests, diseases, and adverse environmental factors that affect their behavior and ability to produce honey. In order for a colony of honey bees to produce honey, they must have an appropriate population peak before the major bloom period in their area. Otherwise, as some old-time beekeepers put it, "They build on the honey flow"—that is, they ramp up brood production rather than store honey. Having the colony peak just before a honey flow means they have the largest possible adult population able to take advantage of the flow, rather than spend it on the young. Optimal management of a honey bee colony depends on both the beekeeper's skill and the quality of the queen's genetics.

Timely hive management is essential to optimal honey production and can mean the difference between a mediocre and a great honey crop. It starts with good fall management for successful wintering, proper and timely spring buildup of the colony and swarm control, and good brood production from the queen, all the while making sure there is more than adequate food available—whether supplied by Mother Nature or the beekeeper—to keep everybody well fed. Putting colonies in locations with a bounty of floral sources; timing the harvest so there's always room in the hive; and handling the harvested crop with care and caution all matter to the quality, purity, and amount of the honey harvested.

For example, beeswax comb that's old can be loaded with residues of propolis, dust and environmental debris, and pollen that stain the surface of the wax and can even be absorbed into the wax. When new honey is stored in darkly stained beeswax cells, some of the residue can be absorbed into the honey, altering the flavor and the color. Wise beekeepers replace old combs with a new clean foundation every two or, at most, three years to avoid that. Careful beekeepers also avoid harvesting frames of honey that aren't fully ripened, or cured, to avoid mixing in nectar with high moisture content, which leads to fermentation. Using too much smoke or strong-smelling chemicals to usher the bees away from the frames in order to harvest the honey can lend a lingering burned or chemical flavor to the honey. And certainly the cleanliness of all of the equipment used is important—first, because honey is a food product, but also because soiled equipment, dirty storage tanks, or dusty surroundings can change the quality of the crop.

When and how honey is handled before, during, and after harvest can mean the difference between a honey crop that expresses its terroir and one that erases all traces of it.

Designating Terroir for Honey

In the European Union, terroir is closely associated with the tradition of identifying certain foods and honeys with the region where they are produced. This practice began in the fifteenth century, when the French parliament first set the standards to regulate Roquefort cheese. They

declared that only those cheeses that were aged in the natural Combalou caves of Roquefort-sur-Soulzon could officially be named Roquefort. Although Roquefort-style cheese can be made in other places, it is the crumbly texture and distinctive flavors of sweet, smoky, and salty tang that are closely associated with the region where true Roquefort is produced. Throughout the E.U. and other parts of the world, specialty foods, wines, and honeys are recognized by the place where they are made. These regional foods include some honeys that are protected by a highly respected, legal certification system of labeling products, known as Geographic Indications (GI). This system is similar to the system of appellations used to identify where wine grapes are grown.

In order to be considered for the GI label, foods must meet all of the following government standards: They must be produced by traditional methods, possess certain characteristics, and enjoy a signature reputation as a result of the geographic region where they are produced. Geographic Indications are directly linked to a territory and the unique elements that sustain them. GI also raises consumer awareness and appreciation of regional products, reduces unfair

competition from inferior copies, and helps producers secure premium prices for their goods.

Within the GI are three distinct regimes—Protected Designation of Origin (PDO), which protects the area or region where a food is produced; Protected Geographical Indication (PGI), which protects the name of the area or place where the product is produced; and Traditional Specialty Guaranteed (TSG), which designates the style or tradition of the product. These names have been in use since 1992 and are respected by the international community, except in the United States. Geographic Indication protection is directly associated with terroir in Europe and serves as a an official classification for products that meet those detailed standards.

There are honeys from Portugal, Italy, Spain, Greece, and France that have secured this recognition, as they are named after the region in which they were produced. The coveted Corsica honey of France is GI protected proclaiming the diverse vegetation on the island. Every bottle of honey is analyzed for quality and sensory standards and can be traced to a specific locale and date of harvest. These nectar sources are chestnut, citrus, and spring and autumn maquis (scrubland) honey. The Miele della Lunigiana, or Lunigiana honey, produced in the mountainous region of Tuscany along the Po River, follows strict traditional regulations of the Denominazione di Origine Protetta (DOP), or Controlled Designation of Origin. It is the first honey in Italy to be awarded the DOP status by the European Union. Lunigiana honey is produced from the local nectar of the acacia, chestnut, and wildflowers of this pristine region.

In the United States the only protection available for products, agricultural or otherwise, is in the form of a trademark issued by the U.S. Patent and Trademark Office (USPTO). This type of protection is identified not as a geographic indication but simply as ownership of a name that might happen to be a city or region. Philadelphia Cream Cheese and Chicago deep-dish pizza are foods associated with specific regions. These names act as a trademark, which simply declares ownership of the name and does not refer to the unique sensory qualities of the foods produced in these regions.

Nevertheless, beekeepers in the United States are beginning to proclaim terroir for their honey, some by numbering each jar to correspond with the hive from which it was harvested. Dates are also beginning to appear on labels stating when a honey was harvested and bottled in an effort to offer full disclosure to customers. Some beekeepers have begun to use zip codes, city names, and even street names to identify their honeys, offering traceability for every bottle. Rather than trying to establish a national definition of honey, savvy beekeepers are defining their honey by its location, embracing the concept of terroir. Differentiating their own honey from the sea of commercial honeys that exists serves to better inform the consumer and potentially protect buyers from cheap or illegal imports that may not be pure honey at all. Could we be returning to the practices of the ancient Egyptians of naming the beekeeper as the "sealer of the honey"?

CHAPTER }3

THE HONEY PLANTS

Honey bees forage for food, water, and propolis in all combinations of land-use places—forests; meadows; abandoned fields; city gardens and parks; commercial row-crop farms; orchards; forage crops and feed lots; uncut roadsides; government land of all kinds; backyard vegetable, fruit, and flower gardens; vacant city lots; botanical gardens; street trees; anywhere a honey bee can fly. These locations may be vast monocultures of the same species of plant all blooming at once or a continuously blooming mixed bag of plants.

There are fewer than a thousand commercial beekeepers in the United States, and most of them run their operations as a combination migratory pollination and honey production business. Very few can make a living simply producing honey. Perhaps three or four thousand beekeepers run much smaller operations—a few hundred colonies—and focus on honey production, with perhaps a seasonal pollination contract or two for extra cash. These beekeepers seek opportunities for single-source honeys and produce much of those products.

However, by far the majority of the beekeepers in the United States operate medium- to small-scale operations as hobbyists —maybe as many as fifty colonies but usually far fewer. For the most part, they keep their bees in a single location all, or at least most, of the time. As a rule, those beekeepers tend to harvest only once a season, because harvesting means assembling all the equipment necessary and using a space—a garage, basement, or kitchen—for a short but disruptive time. The all-season honey is a blend of all of the nectars the bees collected during the season. Early willows and dandelions, mid-season clovers and lindens, and late-season goldenrods and asters. Far too often this honey is labeled "wildflower" because the beekeeper has no clue what

FIREWEED

nectars contribute to the final product.

Other small beekeepers, with a keen eye for marketing and a desire to reap more profit, may harvest more than once a year and are able to discriminate their harvests. Early-season honey tends toward light and mild flavors; later honeys are usually bolder, but not too bold, while autumn honeys, if there are autumn honeys, produce stronger flavors and darker colors. So, rather than have a blended, all-season honey with a less distinguishable, identifiable flavor and medium to medium dark color, these beekeepers might have three or more honeys to sell over the course of a season.

The cleverest beekeepers pay close attention to what plants are blooming when and are often able to harvest single-source honeys right from their backyards or rooftops. This is difficult; it requires precise timing and mostly luck. It is extremely rare to find a location where lots and lots of only one plant blooms at a time. When lindens bloom in early summer in a city, for example, other plants bloom at the same time, of course; the nectar flow from hundreds, perhaps thousands, of all these common street trees is overwhelming, and the vast majority of the nectar collected in a short burst will come from many different trees.

Specialized, market-oriented beekeepers move their hives to locations with an abundance of a single type of plant, so that the bees have little choice of diet for a short period of time. For instance, colonies may be moved to recently logged mountainsides in the northwest part of the country to take advantage of the explosion of fireweed bloom that follows in the wake of forest removal, whether by fire, hence the name, or by logging, a far more common event. Forest floors tend to be barren of almost all other plant life because forest owners systematically remove competitive plants, and the lucky few that escape chemical sterilization are usually so shaded that they cannot survive.

BLUEBERRY

Once the trees are gone, sunlight returns and long dormant seeds, unencumbered by herbicides and competition for water and light, spring to life. Fireweed is almost always the first to take advantage of this in abundance, and it suddenly covers acres and acres of once forested hillsides.

Agricultural crops also lend themselves to this single-source honey harvest. Imagine vast acreages of cotton in several states in the Southeast and South and to some degree still in California. There are large citrus groves in Florida, Texas, New Mexico, Arizona, and especially California. The Midwest has huge tracts of soybeans, along with alfalfa for animal feed, and government land—almost all of North Dakota is government land—is covered in sweet clover as far as you can see.

Only Maine has wild, or low-bush, blueberries of any abundance, but other states such as Georgia, Michigan, and Florida produce high-bush blueberries as a crop and, though similar, cropped blueberry honey is not the same as the wild nectar from Maine. Only Massachusetts and Wisconsin produce enough cranberries to make a cranberry honey crop, but apple honey is produced on the East Coast from the Virginias all the way to Maine and westward, in places, to the Rockies, and especially in the Pacific Northwest. Cane crops, including raspberries and blackberries, are abundant in the Northwest, too, both as a crop and essentially as a weed.

Like politics, all honey is local, and a key player in honey production, and a honey's terroir, is the weather. Consider black locust honey. When the black locust blooms in the

United States, from early April to late May, south to north, it is, unfortunately, almost never the only blooming plant in a honey bee's world. Add to this the fact that concurrently blooming plants may differ from year to year because of the weather. A warm and early spring compresses the bloom of dandelions (*Taraxacum officinalis*), tulip poplar (*Liriodendron spp.*), and cane plants (*Rubus spp.*), so they all bloom early and at once rather than in intervals. When this occurs, the locust, which will still bloom at its normal time, has a subtle but different nectar mix in its final product. Likewise, a cool spring may cause some of these plants to bloom later than normal, so they peak after the locust bloom, again affecting the mix of nectars available at any one time.

LINDEN

Like politics, all honey is local, and a key player in honey production, and a honey's terroir, is the weather.

A honey's terroir, then, that sense of place from which the nectar that makes the honey is gathered, is created in part not only by where the plants grow but also by when they bloom and the weather in a given year.

To add to the confusion, similar plants are often grouped together and considered the same even though the honeys they produce are not identical. This is especially true with perennial and orchard crops. Often the "sameness" of the plants tends to fool us. For instance, when a label says Orange Blossom Honey, in all likelihood it is a mix of orange, lemon, lime, grapefruit, and tangerine. Since they all taste similar, they are often labeled with an easy-to-identify name. "Citrus" just doesn't have the same caché.

Weather extremes can affect the honey.

Plants growing in conditions of extreme heat or drought one season, when they normally experience neither condition, may produce nectar with a slightly different mix of components than usual. The resulting honey may be sweeter or less sweet depending on the ability of the plant to manufacture essential sugars and other components, including the volatiles, enzymes, and color compounds. A typical single-source clover honey may be light in color one year, with a predictably average flavor; while the next year it may be a tad darker, thicker, and more robust in flavor, which is very unclover-like, all because of a weather anomaly.

In the remaining pages of this chapter, we have outlined some of the better-known honey plants that provide the most easily found and most exciting single-source honeys and described what makes each of them special and unique. The terroir—the soil, the weather, and the terrain in which the plant grows—plays a distinct role in the character of each single-source honey. But opportunity for the nectars to be mixed with other floral sources by the honey bees is always present and is often overlooked when it comes to distinguishing honeys. We will shed some light on that aspect of the flavor, too.

We've also included some of the lesser-known sources—rare in abundance perhaps, or seldom found outside a particular region, or simply obscure as a honey and not often promoted as a single-source delight. We invite you to seek out all of these delicacies in your quest for the perfect honey—the common and the rare, the bold and the meek.

FAMILY *Fabaceae*

GENUS *Medicago*

SPECIES *sativa*

OTHER NAME *lucerne*

ALFALFA

Alfalfa, a member of the pea family, like black locust, clover, and soybeans, is the highest-quality and highest-yield hay crop for beef and dairy cattle, horses, sheep, and goats grown anywhere in the world. It originated in the Mideast, and about 20 million acres of it are grown annually in the United States, the world's largest producer, much of it west of the Mississippi River but almost as much in the eastern United States. Seed production is primarily on the West Coast under irrigation because of low humidity, neutral soil, and reduced pest and disease pressure. But both the availability of irrigation water and the quality of that water remain a limiting factor in increasing seed production.

Alfalfa is a perennial herb, living anywhere from four to eight years, depending on variety and area grown. It grows to about three feet tall and has an incredibly deep root system, allowing it to thrive where other forage plants fail due to seasonal droughts. Farmers cut it three to twelve times a season and bale or chop it for future use. It is highly digestible, has a high protein content, and is the fifth-largest crop grown in the United States behind corn, soybeans, wheat, and cotton. It is estimated that more than 400 million tons of alfalfa hay are produced annually in the world to feed hungry animals.

As a result of the vast acreage, alfalfa honey is common, but not as common as you might think. As an alfalfa plant develops, it distributes its protein compounds to the leaves slowly at first, then rapidly, and then slowly as the plant matures. The protein in the leaves reaches its highest concentration just as flower buds begin to form and reaches its peak when about 10 percent of the flowers on the plant are open. That's when farmers harvest the crop, cutting it to let it regrow for another cutting in two or three months. So beekeepers don't get to harvest nearly as much honey from this crop as they would like. Sometimes, when the weather doesn't cooperate, farmers can't or won't cut the crop as early as they'd like, and lucky nearby beekeepers can harvest the bounty.

ALFALFA HONEY TASTING NOTES

VEGETAL WOODY FLORAL

Loaded with personality, alfalfa honey is not as humble as the name implies. This quintessential table honey is a cream-colored light amber with greenish gray or sometimes a tint of orange hues. It can be described as full bodied and reasonably clear. Its aroma is warm with notes of straw, cinnamon, and spice. It has a flavor profile that is clearly identifiable as dry hay and grass clippings, but with a bite. Assertive and persistent, the flavors come to you at the start, then linger on your tongue and leave a burning in the back of the throat that honey lovers welcome. Alfalfa has flavors that are showier, crisper, and more fragrant than those of other vegetal honeys yet pleasant enough for every palate.

This honey pairs well with a warm slice of corn bread, polenta, or grits. It also inspires cravings for brie or herb-crusted Cabra Romero cheese and flatbread crackers. Wash it down with an Indian pale ale, pinot blanc, or chamomile tea.

APPLE BLOSSOM

FAMILY *Rosaceae*
GENUS *Malus*
SPECIES *domestica*

Apple orchard management is rapidly changing. It used to be that apple growers would plant many varieties of apples in their orchards, with five or six rows of one variety planted next to a row of another variety and a few pollinizers mixed in every tenth tree or so in every row. This arrangement was necessary because apples are not self-fruitful. That is, to make an apple, one variety of apple blossom requires pollen from a different variety of apple blossom to set fruit. It takes Gala pollen to produce McIntosh apples, for example.

Just before bloom, honey bee colonies were brought to these mixed orchards, and it was assumed that when the bees visited the blossoms, they would transfer the pollen from that Gala blossom to that McIntosh blossom as they went from tree to tree down the row.

Mostly though, a honey bee will visit only one tree, rarely two, on a foraging trip, so she contacts only Gala blossoms as opposed to moving from Gala to McIntosh. However, when that Gala forager returns home, she still has Gala pollen all over her. As she moves around inside the hive, she might rub against another forager who happens to have been visiting a McIntosh tree, and pollen from each gets transferred. Then when our Gala forager goes back to that Gala tree carrying a little bit of McIntosh pollen — voila! A Gala apple happens.

Look closely at a blooming apple branch, however, and you'll see that there is one blossom on the tip of the branch and several more, maybe as many as six or ten, blossoms on the branch behind it. If each blossom is pollinated, each fruit will be average size. If only the blossom on the tip of the branch, called the king blossom, gets pollinated, there will be far fewer apples on that tree, but, boy, will they be big. Today, apple growers don't want a tree to produce hundreds of average-size apples. Apple money isn't in how many apples one grows but rather in how big the individual apples are.

Apple trees have changed, too. Growers don't plant huge trees anymore. Today's apple trees are scrawny things, propped up with posts and wires and trellises and pruned to produce only a very few fruiting branches. So not only are apple growers interested in just the king blossom, but there are fewer king blossoms to pollinate on each tree. However, there will be ten to fifty times more trees in the orchard.

As a result of this major shift in orchard management, honey bee behavior has changed, as well. It used to be that honey bees would spend ten days to two weeks in an orchard, depending on the weather, but in these new orchards it takes only two, maybe four, days for the bees to get the king blossoms pollinated and punch out.

You can therefore imagine what has happened to the supply of apple blossom honey. It's been reduced by two thirds, maybe more. It's almost impossible to find, and there's another problem. Apple blossoms produce nectar mostly in the morning, which means that bees will visit another plant, likely dandelions, in the afternoon. If the orchard is large enough, you can get a honey that is mostly apple, but it will almost always have something else mixed in.

Some dedicated orchard managers will go the extra mile to remove all the other blossoms, including berries, dandelions, and other fruit blossoms, essentially denying the bees anything else to forage upon, and in so doing will keep the honey in their hives purely apple blossom honey. The honey is worth the effort.

APPLE BLOSSOM HONEY TASTING NOTE

This early spring honey is harvested months before the fall apple-picking season. Apple blossom honey glows auburn in color, with blushing crimson highlights that will remind you of last autumn's apple cider, until it crystallizes into a much lighter straw yellow.

If paler green hues are present, they could be due to those dandelions blooming around the edge of the orchard. The aroma is soft spoken, so you'll have to dip your nose deep into the jar to gather any trace of the musty cider fragrance.

On the tongue, you'll sense the honey's velvety texture and full body. Sweet but not cloying, fruity yet tart, the flavor notes introduce themselves upfront, and the smooth sweetness lingers into a caramelized candy apple finish that lingers.

A chewy, nutty cheddar cheese served with freshly sliced apples and walnuts satisfies this honey. Serve with a chilled Riesling, champagne, or honeyed mead that will brighten up this honey's cider notes. For a quick snack spread some tahini with sesame seeds or crunchy sunflower butter over

FRUIT SPOILED WARM

freshly sliced apples and drizzle with apple honey. Use it to glaze a warm tarte tatin fresh from the oven or mix it into a honey mustard dressing.

AVOCADO

FAMILY *Lauraceae*

GENUS *Persea*

SPECIES *americana*

COMMON NAMES alligator pear

This tropical and Mediterranean climate, medium to tall, long-lived tree is originally native to central Mexico but has been shared with all parts of the world that have a similar climate. Avocados favor well-aerated soil and do not tolerate salt. They are related to cinnamon and the bay laurel, and the fruit is actually a large berry with a single seed. They do well in the United States from Texas to California, plus Florida and Hawaii.

Long-lived is not an overstatement when applied to avocados. Some of the old masters in Mexico reach sixty feet tall, and the oldest are more than four hundred years old, often with no signs of slowing down. They seem to have no set life span and have to be killed rather than die of natural causes.

California produces 90–95 percent of the U.S. avocado crop, with about 59,000 acres under cultivation, harvesting about 300 million pounds of fruit, 60 percent of which comes from San Diego County. There are several varieties, differing in oil content, cold hardiness, outer skin color, mature plant shape, size, and fruiting age; but one variety, Hass, dominates the market, representing about 80 percent of the world's production.

Even though the creamy, nutty-flavored fruit is appealing, for a honey lover it's the flowers that command attention. There are actually two kinds of flowers, but only one kind is on any one tree. Avocado production centers on whether a tree has an "A" or a "B" type flower.

Here's the difference. On day one of a blossom's two-day cycle, a flower on a tree with A-type opens as a female, ready to accept pollen from a blossom from another tree, but only for a short while, because it closes by late morning or early afternoon. It remains closed the rest of the first day, all evening, and the morning of the second day. Then it opens in the early afternoon of the second day as a male flower, with its anthers dehiscing pollen like there was no tomorrow. And that's because, as far as this flower is concerned, there is no tomorrow. It sheds pollen until it closes at dusk, and thus ends that blossom's productive life. If it was able to gather pollen during that first day as a female flower, it would be able to set fruit. If not, it withers and falls to the ground.

A tree with B-type flowers follows a different path. On day one of its bloom cycle the flower quietly waits until just after noon to open as a female and then accepts pollen from any avocado tree shedding pollen at the moment. It remains receptive for the rest of the day and then closes for the evening. Early the next morning it awakens and opens as a male flower, shedding pollen—you guessed it—like there is no tomorrow, because, as with its cousin, there is no tomorrow. You can see that in a grove of avocado trees the greatest number of female flowers is available when the greatest number of male flowers is available—from just before to just after noon—which also happens to be the best time of day for a honey bee to fly.

So you can see why honey bees are so important to avocado production. A blossom cannot pollinate itself, and no blossom on a tree can pollinate any other blossom on the same tree. For a blossom to set fruit, pollen from another tree, of a different variety, must travel from the anthers of one flower to the pistil of another flower hitching its ride on a honey bee. That is why growers plant an alternate variety of tree in almost every row, and why avocado blossoms are such profuse nectar producers. They have to reward honey bees very handsomely to get them to visit and to keep them visiting. Flowers are borne on two- to three-inch stalks off buds on a branch, with ten to twelve stalks emanating from each bud. Panicles of blossoms are produced along each stalk and are bunched at the tip. Each stalk may have twenty to thirty individual blossoms. In fact, a mature avocado tree will produce a million or more blossoms in the spring, almost all of which wither and fall to the ground, failing to produce fruit. Yet a healthy tree in a good location may produce from one hundred to two hundred avocados, from a million blossoms.

Blossoms are small, one quarter by one half inch or so. They are fragile, susceptible to drying winds, low humidity, and even the lightest frost. Poor pollination and early fruit drop are common when those environmental extremes occur.

A number of years ago, far-thinking investors saw a future in investing in avocado production. But in Southern California, prime, and even average, cropland is expensive, and hillside land is very inexpensive; so investors instructed their growers to purchase all the cheap hillside land they could find and start planting avocado trees as fast as they could. For a half dozen years or so they waited. When the trees were finally ready to produce fruit, the growers realized that they needed a way to get honey bees to the trees in order to pollinate them. Unfortunately, the large trucks, forklifts, and pallets used to transport the beehives did not do well on 45 degree hillsides. The investments were going to go for ruin if something wasn't done. To the rescue came beekeepers with ancient equipment, old-time booms from fifty or more years ago, used for moving one colony at a time. They worked perfectly on the hillsides. Those boom-bearing

beekeepers knew how essential they were to the avocado-growing operation, and today bee colony rental for those avocado plantations is at a premium and beekeepers who have the old-time equipment are doing well. What's more, they are helping to produce tons of delicious avocado honey.

AVOCADO HONEY TASTING NOTES

FRUIT WOODY WARM

For those who like warm, smoky flavors, avocado honey delivers a deep, fruity tasting experience. There is a remote vegetal note in this honey that will remind you, not surprisingly, of an avocado, with the smooth-as-butter mouth feel to match. Avocado honey is a dark amber color, close to a hazelnut. The aroma is slightly lactic, reminiscent of cooked butter and warm chestnut. The texture is silky on the tongue but dissolves rather quickly. You'll find woody, smoky, burnt sugar, and caramel notes that mellow into brown sugar or maple syrup.

Avocado honey pairs well with the earthy, nutty flavors of Mousseron du Jura cheese, with dried apricots and a glass of syrah. It makes an excellent glaze for a baked ham. Drizzle it over a crispy pear and bacon empanada or to finish a chili con carne. This honey is also a great substitute for maple syrup. Drizzle liberally over fresh mangos or your breakfast bacon or sausage.

BLACK LOCUST

FAMILY *Fabaceae*

GENUS *Robinia*

SPECIES *pseudoacacia*

OTHER NAMES locust, acacia, false acacia

The black locust tree is almost as interesting as the black locust honey beekeepers work so hard to obtain. There are varieties with dangerously long and incredibly sharp thorns on the trunk and especially the branches, even down to the tips of twigs. Some selections have been made to eliminate those, so if you choose to grow black locust as a timber crop or as a specimen tree, look for a thornless variety. The wood is dense and rot resistant and makes excellent fence posts or outdoor timbers; it has been raised as a timber crop because of that for centuries. But it is also commonly used in home and city landscapes because of the fragrant flowers, and, because its autumn leaves are small, they decompose quickly and do not clutter gutters and lawns.

Native to the east central United States, black locust has been transported to nearly every part of the temperate world. Great stands exist in Europe, especially eastern and southern Europe, east to China, and all across the United States, with the exception of the desert South and Southwest and high-altitude mountains.

Because of this they have escaped cultivation and have become invasive in many locations. But the locust borer beetle has had the most influence on the spread of this tree. The adult lays eggs on the base of the trunk; the larvae tunnel inside and within a season will kill the host tree by destroying the water transport system in the trunk. The locust responds by sending out a great many suckers from the existing roots, setting up clumps of locust trees whenever this happens. By killing one, the borer actually propagates the host. Don't you love the irony?

Adding to the irony, the adult locust borer, a beautiful black and yellow long-horned beetle, is a floral companion of honey bees in the autumn because both find the pollen and nectar of goldenrod flowers a rare treat in the late season; they are commonly seen on the flowers together.

The extremely showy, brilliantly white, pendulous flower clusters appear from April to June, depending on latitude, with anywhere from forty to one hundred individual pea-shaped, extremely fragrant florets in a cluster. It appears that the number of florets in a cluster is somewhat dependent on the weather during the previous season. Ample moisture helps to produce many flowers the following season, while dry summers can re-

The Honey Plants

59

duce flower count significantly. If the winter preceding bloom is severe, the bloom may be reduced, but it's anybody's guess most years.

Producing a locust honey crop is never a given. Long-time beekeepers in the eastern United States will tell you that even when locust trees are laden with bloom, a good honey crop may be had only one year in seven; but on average they will make a fair to small crop three years out of seven. You can almost bet that it will be rainy some days of bloom no matter where you are, and one or two years in seven a late freeze will destroy what promised to be a prosperous crop. Some seasons the flowers just don't show up for what appears to be no reason at all. Beekeepers consider locust honey a bonus, not a predictable moneymaker.

But when the locusts are in bloom, everybody within a half mile knows because of the almost sickly sweet but not heavy fragrance that seems to drift across lawns, city streets, and open meadows on even the slightest breeze. If you happen to be near a clump of trees, you may notice that their blooming dates, start to finish, and density of blooms are identical. It's uncanny. And overpowering.

Because of its bloom schedule, it is not difficult to obtain a pure, varietal locust honey. In the eastern United States, the most obvious spoiler is tulip poplar, which gives it a darker, reddish tint and may change the flavor slightly. There may be a few other intruders, such as Russian olive, which may bloom at the same time; and some of the early fruit tree, raspberry, or blackberry blooms may interfere, but mostly black locust, will stand alone if it's a productive year.

There is an imposter, of sorts. Often you'll see an expensive, exotic, single-source honey labeled "Acacia," usually an import, usually from Europe, and very often from Italy. This is not a honey produced from one of the acacia (Acacia sp.) trees found in the southern and western United States and many other countries. No, it is honey from the common black locust tree, imported from the United States. Occasionally, it is lighter than a typical single-source black locust honey, but more often it is the same water white you are used to. Flavor? The darker offerings do not reflect the taste of black locust honey at all; there is definitely a second, maybe a third, honey involved. A clear white "acacia" honey will be similar but not quite the same. It may seem the tiniest bit different, with just a bit of a heavier, drier mouth feel.

BLACK LOCUST HONEY TASTING NOTES

FRUIT
WARM
SPOILED

Hard to find, and unreliable most years, black locust honey is one of the premier honeys in the temperate climate world. In its purest form it is known for a subtle delicacy in both its fragrance and its flavor. The gorgeous pale yellow straw color is water white on the honey color chart and transparent as glass and is attractive to consumers who associate this quality with a premium honey product. When you open a jar of locust honey, aromatic notes of beeswax and pineapple immediately fill the air. Occasionally a slight hint of fermentation can be detected in the aroma, but that taste does not appear on the tongue (unless the honey is actually fermented). Silky in texture, the flavors recall mellow butterscotch, almonds, and vanilla, but not immediately. You will have to savor each spoonful and recognize them at the finish. These flavor notes tend to be much more distinct in the black locust's popular European sister, acacia.

Pair either of these honeys with a firm, salty cheese such as a Pecorino Romano or provolone and a glass of chardonnay. Black locust is a stellar choice for drizzling over a fruit and custard butter tart or toasted almond ice cream.

The Honey Connoisseur

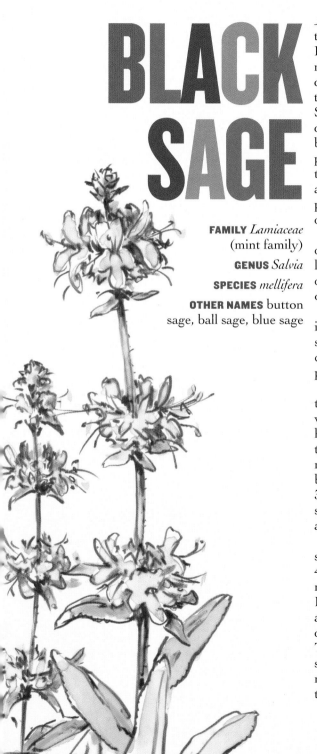

BLACK SAGE

FAMILY *Lamiaceae* (mint family)

GENUS *Salvia*

SPECIES *mellifera*

OTHER NAMES button sage, ball sage, blue sage

From a beekeeper's perspective and a talented honey connoisseur's experience, all of the honeys discussed on these pages range from terrific to fantastic. From a horticulturist's perspective, though, many of the plants these wonderful honeys originate from are imports or brash imposters posing as productive citizens. Not sage. Sage carries with it the native charm of the old American West, the romance of cowboys, chaparral, and ghost towns, of desert panoramas and lonesome landscapes. It has the fragrance and beauty of both foliage and flower that make it a garden gem, the perfect pollinator partner, and the object of desire everywhere it grows.

And sage honey? For more than a hundred years it has stirred the souls of honey lovers around the world, and it can be produced only from the dry, rocky coastal hills of western and Southern California.

Although there are many species of sage, including sagebrush, white sage, purple sage, chaparral yucca, manzanita, and even creosote bush, it's black sage that leads the pack in quality, quantity, and reputation.

Black sage is a perennial shrub that grows three to six feet tall and about the same width. It is highly aromatic; thousands of hairs on both sides of the leaves and on the typically square stems give off that sagey, minty, wonderful smell when brushed or broken. It grows from sea level to about 3,500–4,000 feet above sea level, where sagebrush, a sage imposter takes over; shear altitude is one good way to tell them apart.

Black sage thrives on sandstone, shale, serpentine, and basalt soils, with a pH of 4–8. It is adaptable to most any soil environment with those minimum requirements. Roots penetrate to about two feet but mostly are in the top five inches of soil, so the plant doesn't have access to deeper soil moisture. This means that it can be out-competed by some of its neighbors in dry years. Under normal conditions it lives to be fifteen to twenty years old.

Black sage is openly, even loosely, branched and spreads easily; it uses prostrate limbs to send out roots at nodes, seed dispersal, and adventitious stalks that spring up from the shallow root crown. It is sensitive to soil moisture, needing something like fifteen inches of rain a year to thrive. If less rain falls, the plant sheds its leaves to save moisture, which diminishes or eliminates bloom the following year, a habit that is bothersome to beekeepers. It sends out most of its annual growth after autumn rains, if there are autumn rains, its blossom stems shoot up the next spring. It has some allelopathic tendencies—that is, it inhibits the growth of nearby competing plants—and is aggressive when pioneering newly disturbed soil or burned areas, though serious fires can destroy the shallow roots. Because it spreads by both seeds and shoots, it tends to produce rather dense stands of multiple-aged plants, competing nicely with its chaparral neighbors, even taking over some of the partial shade areas between taller plants.

The leaves are dark green and wrinkled on top, but nearly white underneath. Flowers appear from April to July, depending on altitude and last year's abundance of rainfall, with a typical mint family floral arrangement. That is, the stalk shoots up to three or four feet tall, and at every node, not leaves but blossoms appear, their greenish sepals clinging tightly to the stem and completely surrounding the stalk, forming a button or ball at each node. The half-inch pale blue to white flowers begin to appear at the bottom of the stalk and mature upward as the lower blossoms go to seed. Honey bees and many other insects seek out this incredibly rich source of nectar and pollen, providing pollination in their search. Once the blossoms have been fertilized, they remain on the stem, slowly turning black by season's end, hence the "black" in black sage.

Black sage provides habitat and food for wildlife; plus, it is excellent to use for erosion control and as an ornamental in the xeric landscape.

It tends to be a somewhat unreliable honey producer, some years providing hundreds of pounds of honey for nearby colonies but other years hardly any at all. As noted, previous rainfall is one factor, but bloom-time weather can also be detrimental, coastal fog being a real troublemaker in some years.

As a member of the *Salvia* genus, black sage has some medicinal value, not unlike many mints, in relieving coughs and congestion, and it can be used to make teas and for flavoring. But it is the white, heavy-bodied honey, which doesn't granulate, that is prized worldwide.

SAGE HONEY TASTING NOTES

SPOILED WOODY ANIMAL FRUIT

Deeply rich and complex in flavors, sage honey is water white transparent with a warm cocoa tint. Its aroma is of balsamic and resins that remind you of crushed sage leaves. This honey is full bodied and velvety, so lush that it practically hugs your tongue. You need just one taste to discover how luxurious it is. There are many layers of flavor, beginning with a sweet and smoky candied fruit, fig, and butterscotch and ending with a camphorous kick of cool menthol. There is a twinge of bitterness to sage honey that adds an interesting edge to the impressive mix.

Pair sage honey with a salty fontina cheese, rustic olive oil bread, and a glass of Chianti. Drizzle over pappardelle with lemon and mushrooms, roasted potatoes, or cauliflower or mix into a watermelon sage martini. Sage honey makes a perfect accompaniment to butter on cornmeal biscuits.

BLACKBERRY

FAMILY *Rosaceae*
GENUS *Rubus*
SPECIES *fruticosus*
OTHER NAMES wild blackberry, brambles, canes

There are several types of brambles—raspberries, dewberries, loganberries, and the like—but when it comes to popularity and dominance in size and sheer numbers, common blackberries are king. They grow in temperate climates and have escaped into the wild everywhere they have been introduced as a domestic crop. It's common to see them growing on the edges of forests, roads, and streams or in abandoned fields and ditches and on unused land, anywhere there is moderate- to well-drained, slightly acidic soil, and mostly full sunlight. They don't tolerate wet feet, however, so there is at least one limiting factor.

Blackberry plants are perennial, with the same habit as all brambles, of producing biennial stems, or canes, hence their other general name—cane fruit. First-year canes, called primocanes, are new stems, emanating from the root crown or more likely from a rooted node from another first-year cane that either crept along the ground, which

is common, or sprang up from the tip of a cane that grew up high and then bent over, the tip rooting where it touched the ground, which is equally common. Primocanes produce lateral buds and branches that ultimately produce flowers in the second year. Depending on location, primocanes will be anywhere from 10 to 20 feet long, with large leaves. Large canes can be 4 to 6 inches in diameter at the base.

The second year, the cane becomes a floricane. It doesn't grow longer, but all those lateral buds and branches produce flowering lateral branches as well as leaves, which are smaller than in the first year.

When unimpeded, groups of canes can grow into a large, dense thicket. A hedge two rows deep can stop a car. When left to their own devices in an open area, they can produce thickets 12 to 15 feet tall, covering an acre or more of land. Flame throwers, dynamite, and gallons of herbicide will subdue such an impenetrable barrier but only with difficulty. Thickets of this size are far more common in the West than the Midwest or the eastern United States, but wherever they grow, these thickets can be imposing.

The five-petal flowers are produced in late spring or early summer. They are classic rose family flowers, an inch or so across, and grow in bunches of ten to twenty or more. They are typically white to light pink, with a large number of individual center pistals surrounded by an equally great number of anther-topped styles. The nectary is below the surface of the flower, between the styles and the pistals. Some types of blackberries are self-fertile (their anthers are bent inward, nearly touching the center pistal to accomplish fertilization). But most need pollen from another plant, pollen transported by honey bees and other pollinators, to reproduce; those blackberries are easily spotted because their anthers point away from the center of the flower. Blackberries happen to require a lot of honey bees to accomplish the task of pollination, so the plant needs to make itself very attractive to honey bees. Not only is there a lot of pollen to be had in every flower, but the nectar from the flowers is loaded with sugar and has a strong fragrance, and purple spots in the center of the flowers act as nectar guides, so they're easy for the bees to find, even in an acre-wide patch of tangle.

The fruit of the blackberry plant is actually an aggregate fruit, composed of numerous drupelets, each with a single seed. Look carefully at a blackberry fruit, and you can see the remains of the pistil stem squeezing out between drupelets; there are as many of these little hair-like remains as there are parts of the berry. Sometimes you'll see a berry that's only partially developed, with many of the drupelets missing. This is the result of few bee visitations, thus poor pollination.

Some types of blackberry plants flower all summer long; when domesticated, those are called ever-bearing. With those plants you will see buds, flowers, and unripe and ripe berries on the plant, all at the same time, even on the same cane. Many ever-bearing plants also don't grow those irritating prickles; although those varieties offer less bloody harvests, they often lack the sumptuous flavor of their more dangerous cousins. Interestingly, unripe blackberries turn red before they turn black, so there's a saying: "Blackberries are red when they're green." Keep this in mind when picking your next batch.

Oregon is by far the largest producer of cultivated blackberries because of its absolutely ideal climate of cool, dry summers and easy winters and a perfect blackberry soil. A recent year's harvest was over 60 million pounds. Crops average two to three tons per acre and up to six tons on productive land with good management and pollination. As you can imagine, the same state also leads the rest in blackberry honey production. And though blackberry honey is produced everywhere blackberries grow, the quantity of berries and isolation of the crops are almost never enough to produce pure blackberry honey. Still, any honey that shares even a little of its origins with wild blackberries in the spring is only the better for the experience.

BLACKBERRY HONEY TASTING NOTES

FRUIT WARM FLORAL

A summertime favorite, blackberry honey is loaded with all the sweet and tart flavor notes you look forward to in the berry. At first glance, it's a bit of a surprise that this honey is very light amber with a burnt orange tint if harvested in the Pacific Northwest and a transparent cream tint if it's from the East Coast. Blackberry honey crystallizes quickly, its color turning to near smoky ochre. Beautiful aromas of sweet, bright currants and warm brown sugar escape the newly opened jar. Your tongue will appreciate this honey's smooth butteriness and sticky texture. Overall this honey is mild flavored and delicate with notes of cotton candy, marshmallows, and prunes infused with rich, concentrated blackberry flavor. A refreshing tartness remains on your tongue at the end.

Pair blackberry honey with mascarpone cheese, lavender sprigs, fresh berries, and a glass of merlot. Mix a blackberry honey glaze for salmon or ham. Drizzle it over vanilla bean ice cream with fresh mint or over a sour cream pound cake. Add it to a cool glass of limeade.

BLUEBERRY

FAMILY *Ericaceae*

GENUS *Vaccinium*

SPECIES *cyanococcus,*
angustifolium

OTHER NAMES
highbush blueberry,
lowbush blueberry

U.S. blueberry production is impressive, especially when wild and cultivated harvests are combined. Nearly 430 million pounds of fruit are produced annually. Over 80 million pounds of wild blueberries come from Maine alone, and Michigan picks over 70 million pounds and Oregon nearly 70 million pounds, with New Jersey, California, Florida, and Georgia making up most of the rest.

High-bush blueberries are those under intense, row-crop cultivation. With over 70,000 acres of high-bush blueberries in the United States, there are scores of varieties bred to grow in the South, North, and Midwest; on the West Coast; and everywhere in between. These berries vary in size, color (there's even a pink blueberry), bloom time, and harvest dates. Side by side they are pretty easy to tell apart, and even the flavors differ somewhat.

The cultivated bushes can grow twelve to thirteen feet tall and get to be two to four feet wide. They like a sunny location with sandy loamy soil with a pH of 4–5, good drainage, and lots of organic matter. Because their roots are close to the surface, they need a steady supply of moisture. Most varieties are self-fertile, so blossoms produce a berry if visited by an insect that will transfer the pollen within the flower. This is done by bees generally and honey bees and bumblebees mostly. But when one of those bees visits a flower of another variety first, then shares the pollen from the first flower, the second flower produces a bigger, sweeter berry that has more seeds and ripens sooner. To make sure this happens as often as possible, growers bring in one to two colonies of honey bees for every acre of blueberry plants and generally plant four rows of one variety next to four rows of another variety to get better yields across the field.

Blueberry flowers are unique. They are bell shaped, white to pale pink or red with some green, depending on the variety. But what makes them so unusual is that they need to be "buzz" pollinated. The pollen-producing organs in a blueberry flower are tube-like; when mature, they open at the downward-facing end through a pore. A bumblebee is especially equipped to hang on a flower and vibrate its wing muscles to shake loose the pollen from the tubes inside, which lands on the underside of its abdomen. When the bee visits another flower, it probes deep inside for the nectar, transferring the pollen on its abdomen from the previous flower to the receptive area of the next flower, thus enabling pollination. Honey bees, however, don't buzz- pollinate. Rather, they grab the anther with their legs and shake it, releasing the pollen and accomplishing the same result as the bumblebee, but with slightly more work.

Wild blueberries are grown in several states, but it's Maine that leads the world in production. Maine's wild blueberries grow naturally on what are called the Barrens, the wild, windblown, mostly flat, rocky, high-acid, barely fertile soils of the southeast corner of the state, along the south-facing coast. There are 60,000 acres of wild plants there, but only 30,000 or so acres are harvested each year. Eighty-three million pounds of blueberries are picked off those 30,000 acres, but they're half the size of the berries from their cultivated cousins. How does that happen?

Like cultivated blueberries, wild blueberries produce their best fruit when different varieties are growing close to each other. With wild blueberries, this happens naturally. If you look at a 1,000-acre patch, it's actually easy to see the different varieties, because they vary in color, height, and density. The difference between the wild and cultivated berries is that the wild berry plants are only four inches tall. Four inches!

The wild plants are grown on a two-year cycle, which explains why only half of the 60,000 acres is harvested each year. During year one, plants are encouraged to grow; they are fertilized, watered, and protected from frost, insects, and disease. In May more than 65,000 honey bee colonies are brought in from all the United States to make up the second-largest annual pollination event, exceeded only by California's almond pollination, which takes place each year in February.

It takes more than two colonies on each acre of blueberries to pollinate those 30,000-plus acres. On average, there are 10 million blossoms on every acre, and growers hope for an 80–90 percent fruit set.

The colonies stay approximately one month, with Maine weather, which can be cool, damp, or foggy even in May, sometimes wreaking havoc on pollination. Flowers are open for five to eight days, but they're receptive to fertilization only for the first two or three days. As is the case in their cultivated cousins, the wild flowers are bell-shaped, downward hanging, self-fertile, and in need of an insect to move the pollen.

Harvest is usually over by Labor Day, at which time the plants are burned or mowed to encourage new growth the next season and to control weeds and diseases. In the second season, the plants are recharged and they regrow, but they don't produce blossoms or fruit. All the plant's energy goes into roots, stems, branches, and blossom potential for the next season.

Beekeepers don't make a lot of wild blueberry honey most years, because the fields are so overpopulated with bees that individual colonies make little honey. Of course, the competition encourages aggressive foraging for both pollen and nectar, so those millions of blossoms get visited many times during their two to three days of receptivity.

BLUEBERRY HONEY TASTING NOTES

FRUIT
FLORAL
CITRUS

Both highbush (*cyanococcus*) and lowbush (*angustifolium*) blueberries are native Americans, but there's a discernible difference in the flavor of the two honeys. The flavor of honey from cultivated, overbred, pampered, domesticated high-bush blueberries tends to be much less robust than the honey from the oh-so-sweet Maine and Michigan wild low-bush blueberry honey. It's a difference you'll recognize immediately in a side-by-side taste comparison.

Blueberry blossom honey is no doubt one of the most exciting honeys you will ever taste, because you'll taste blueberries in every spoonful. The color is light amber to medium yellow with a bolt of deep blue, reminiscent of the fruit. The nose of the wild low-bush is distinctively fruity and more blueberry-like than the high-bush. If your honey was harvested in Maine, the color will be deeper blue and will reveal an even more pronounced blueberry flavor than a harvest from, say, New Jersey or Oregon. Blueberry honey will have a smooth, buttery texture that coats your tongue like a silk robe. Along with its blueberry flavor, the notes of violets and jasmine flowers, as well as lemony citrus notes, are impossible to resist.

Drizzle blueberry honey over any goat cheese and garnish with a fresh sprig of mint. Pair it with a sparkling white wine. It also perfectly complements Greek yogurt or muesli, or you can mix it into banana smoothies. This honey is a perfect accompaniment to lemon poppy seed muffins and blueberry cream cheese turnovers.

Buckwheat is an old crop. Records indicate that it was already domesticated in China by 6000 BC. It had moved to central Asia, the Mideast, and Europe by 4000 BC and came to the United States with the colonists. It is still popular in both China and Russia. At one time the United States was growing a million acres of the crop, mostly in the Northeast, primarily in New York and Pennsylvania, but also south to the Carolinas and west to North Dakota. But by the mid-1950s, only 150,000 acres or so were still in existence, and by the mid-1960s, only about 50,000 acres were under cultivation. Today about 70,000 acres are grown, mostly under contract in the Dakotas and Minnesota, with much of that slated for export to Japan. Worldwide only about four million acres are still grown.

FAMILY *Polygonaceae*
GENUS *Fagopyrum*
SPECIES *esculentum*

BUCKWHEAT

Buckwheat is grown as a grain crop for its seeds, which are ground into flour, but it's not in the grass family. Rather, it is related to sorrels and rhubarb. It is a short-season annual, often planted and harvested two or three times from the same field in a season. It is also grown for green manure, to be plowed under to enrich the soil, or as a cover crop to smother weed growth on a piece of land destined for more lucrative crops, where chemical weed control is not acceptable. Conservationists plant it for wildlife food and cover, and it is sometimes used for erosion control on steep roadside banks. It thrives in a moist, cool environment. It grows in infertile and moderately to poorly drained acid soils that are low in available nitrogen.

Buckwheat is planted on harrowed or disturbed soil, grows to three or four feet tall, blooms in five to six weeks, and is ready to harvest in ten to eleven weeks. It has a single stem with branches near the top where the startlingly white blossoms appear. It will continue to grow and produce flowers until it is harvested or freezes. When a field is in blossom, it appears to be covered with snow, but it offers a disagreeable fragrance not appreciated by many people.

The flowers don't have petals, only sepals, and each flower produces a single triangular-shaped seed, an *achene*, much like a sunflower seed. The seeds are high in lysine and several other amino acids. Each flower offers nectar from nectaries located below and between eight pollen-bearing stamens, and honey bees are critical to move pollen from those stamens to the pistal for optimum seed set.

The best nectar production occurs when there is ample soil moisture, days are sunny with little wind, and nights are cool. An acre of buckwheat can produce 150 pounds of dark, strong-flavored honey, but buckwheat flowers produce nectar only during the morning hours. At around noon each day the nectaries cease production, and the remaining nectar evaporates, leaving foraging honey bees irritable until the next morning, when nectar production begins again.

An ambitious beekeeper can produce buckwheat honey for a good portion of the season, especially in the northern temperate climates. Planting buckwheat crops in late June, then again in early July, and a final plot in mid-July will keep the honey bees in nectar from mid-July to just before frost and the goldenrod bloom. Two to four hundred pounds of premium buckwheat honey can be produced on three acres of land, then harvested, and the bees left to collect goldenrod honey, another superlative crop, for overwinter stores.

Buckwheat yields about a thousand pounds of mature seed per acre (enough seed to plant fifty acres the following year), which will produce six to seven hundred pounds of buckwheat flour, the brown-flecked flour commonly used for pancakes, kasha, farina, groats, noodles, and porridge. If worked further, an acre will produce five hundred pounds of highly refined white flour. And though it has been reduced, demand continues for this flour, because buckwheat has no gluten, and those with that allergy continue to seek it out.

BUCKWHEAT HONEY TASTING NOTES

EARTHY MUSTY ANIMAL MALTY

Dark and brooding, buckwheat honey's ebony shade may remind you of motor oil, which can make taking that first sniff of the jar a challenge. Buckwheat does not, in fact, smell like motor oil. Its nose is more that of a musty basement, malty beer, and aged wood furniture. A generous taste, however, will deliver unexpected waves of chocolate malt balls, dark red cherries, and toasted toffee,with only the woody flavor lingering on your tongue. The texture is thick, and the body is heavy. It's interesting to note, however, that there is a variety of Japanese buckwheat called Tokyo that produces a light, mild-flavored honey.

Pair buckwheat honey with the award-winning nutty cheddar, Barely Buzzed, which has an espresso- and lavender-rubbed rind, or a hardy Stilton and a glass of tawny port or the chocolate lovers' dessert wine called Banyuls. Buckwheat is also a fine substitute for maple syrup, so drizzle it liberally on hotcakes, waffles, and mascarpone-filled crepes. It also perfectly complements a double scoop of chocolate hazelnut gelato.

CLOVER FAMILY

Found on every grocery store shelf and at most farm markets, and a staple in every kitchen, clover honey is America's most common single-source honey. Although similar clovers can contribute to this single-source label, white sweet clover, *Melilotus albus*, is king of all the clovers. Great stretches of the heartland, from the Ohio River to the West Coast and from Canada to Oklahoma, are host to this legume. A European introduction, this biennial is the most common clover grown by farmers in the government's Conservation Reserve Program (CRP), a USDA land restoration program administered by the Farm Service Agency that leases marginally useful acres from landowners, then provides cost-sharing assistance to establish approved soil and resource conservation practices. This program involves no small commitment by the owner since the land is leased by the government—and unavailable for crop production—for ten to fifteen years (with some emergency provisions when severe weather events interfere with normal crop production). In the United States more than 30 million CRP acres of subpar land are protected from additional degradation by reducing runoff and protecting ground and surface water from sediment and contamination problems. CRP crops aim to improve the quality of the soil, too, and white sweet clover, like all legumes, provides additional soil nitrogen for crop growth and deep roots for soil penetration and additional organic matter. It also offers food and shelter for wildlife and pollinators.

White sweet clover was once a major source of hay for cattle, and though it has been replaced by more productive and nutritious crops, few plants can beat its soil-building and wildlife habitat capabilities. Add to this the incredible potential it provides beekeepers for a predictable and consumer-friendly single-source honey. Indeed, for the past twenty-five years, more than half of the top-ten honey-producing states have been those with the most CRP land, and most of them have white sweet clover as far as you can see.

In addition, there are thousands more acres of other government and private land covered with white sweet clover because the soils and the climate of most of the Midwest and parts of many states elsewhere seem to have been made just for this crop. There are, conservatively, many millions of acres of this prolific plant, and most of that land provides everything clover needs to produce all the nectar honey bees can collect.

What does clover need to flourish? Not too much, it seems. A moderately sweet soil with some drainage and a minimum amount of organic matter works best, but moist to wet gravelly locations suit it just fine. In fact, clover is extremely good at returning eroded and damaged soils back to fertile and productive land and has been spread far and wide because it heals land previously damaged beyond use for agriculture. It has aggressively escaped to roadsides, open fields, pastures, and almost any recently harrowed, plowed, or torn-up field in the northern two-thirds of the United States, from Ohio to California. It seems to be missing only from the hottest parts of the South and the arid areas of the Southwest.

White sweet clover, in particular, grows best in the Midwest. Because of its abundance and distribution, it blooms at the same time as a host of other honey-producing plants, so the final composition of the honey is directly dependent on where exactly the plants grow and what grows around them. Most commonly in the mix is yellow sweet clover, which blooms just before and at the very beginning of white's bloom. Later bloomers include sunflowers and buckwheat in the vast stretches of the Midwest, and alfalfa and several tree honeys in other areas where white sweet has spread. Pure white sweet clover is not rare, but it's not always the virgin we'd prefer. It does produce, however. Whether it's pure or mixed with other clovers, beekeepers everywhere will tell you that white sweet is their bread and butter—the mortgage maker.

White sweet isn't the only single-source clover honey produced. Just mentioned is its close relative, yellow sweet clover, *Melilotus officinalis*, also routinely planted on CRP land. Like its cousin, it has escaped to many similar but always a bit dryer places to grow. It blooms a tad earlier than white, so a mixed yellow and white planting, which many landowners arrange, has a longer honey-producing period. This strategy also takes some of the gamble out of honey production if there is a spot of bad weather that keeps the bees at home for part of the extended bloom period. But because it blooms just before white, bees may gather bits of other earlier blooming crops with it. The plentiful, fragrant, and prolific Russian olive bloom, or even dandelion, may be a part of the early flow. The result is nearly single-source white and yellow clover, but with a few other bloomers mixed in.

Adding to the range of clover honeys available is the rest of the agriculture clovers planted elsewhere in the United States. Probably the most predominant, especially in the north central section of the country, is lawn clover, usually called white Dutch or just white clover, *Trifolium repens*, another introduced species. Once the source of hay and pasture feed for the dairy and cattle industry, it has been largely replaced by alfalfa and now exists mostly as a volunteer, spreading by rhizomes and seed into pastures and fields—and, of course, your yard.

White clover requires an even sweeter soil than the other clovers and thrives from western Pennsylvania to Iowa and north into Wisconsin and Minnesota, which for a time was called the clover belt because of the incredible honey crops produced there. Now, with more attentive lawn care and turf and pasture management, this clover can be found almost everywhere, and in many places far distant from the CRP breadbasket. It provides the major honey crop harvested by beekeepers. Its honey is considered clover honey, and because of wide distribution and a nearly summer-long bloom it, too, can harbor other honeys in its folds. Basswood is a good example of a cross bloomer, giving single-source white clover honey just a bit of a tangy aftertaste not usually associated with plain white clover honey. Other summer honeys that might mix in include raspberry, alfalfa, some of the thistles, mint, and even other, less common clovers like alsike and red clover. Single-source white Dutch clover honey is a task to find but worth the search, even if some of the best of the Midwest is mixed in.

If you live in the southern part of the United States, your clover honey was probably gathered from crimson clover, *Trifolium incarnatum*. Though an introduced annual, it is planted extensively across the southeastern United States, along roadsides and for soil improvement and erosion control. The honey is similar to other clover honeys in color and flavor, but because it begins growing in the fall and overwinters as a mature plant (it is not hardy in the North), it blooms very early in the season and often overlaps with some of the more exotic honeys of the South, such as holly, tulip poplar, saw palmetto, and even tallow. Mostly pure crimson clover can be difficult to produce, but, like all the clovers, it is worth searching for, even if it has other honeys mixed in.

So the question remains, Which clover is in that clover honey bottle? It's a good bet that it's the king of clovers, white sweet, but most clover honey remains a mystery, and most people are unaware of the secrets it holds. Still, regardless of its source or an occasional visit by other flavors, clover honey remains the cornerstone of available honeys and one of the best single-source varietal honeys on the shelf. Don't overlook it because it's common. Clover honey sets the standard.

CLOVER HONEY TASTING NOTES

ANIMAL VEGETAL FLORAL

Clover honey can vary slightly in color, aroma, and flavor, depending on the region in which it was produced. It's the most common honey found in all types of stores across the entire country. The best clover honey, however, comes from your local beekeeper.

White and yellow sweet clovers in their purest form are the lightest-colored of all the clovers and are harvested in the northern and midwestern states. They tend to have an attractive, transparent straw to yellow color with a buttery yellow or light chartreuse hue. The aroma is vegetal and floral with notes of warm beeswax, dry hay, grass, and cinnamon surrounded by warm flavors of cooked butter and vanilla.

If your clover honey is harvested closer to the East Coast—say, Pennsylvania or New York—expect it to be darker in color because of cross bloomers. Look for brassy and butterscotch colors and a buttery texture. The flavor has warmer caramel, butterscotch, and toffee notes, with distinct beeswax undertones.

Unheated clover honeys crystallize rapidly, but that does not take anything away from the flavor. Generally, you'll welcome the fine-textured granules and smooth texture on your tongue.

Pair your clover honey with a salty Italian Pecorino or creamy English Lancashire cheese with crostini and a glass of Riesling. Clover is a go-to honey; its mild flavor will enhance any food. Toss a spinach salad with sliced pears and walnuts and a clover honey vinaigrette or drizzle the honey over cardamom-spiced tapioca or butter pecan ice cream.

FAMILY *Ericaceae*
GENUS *Vaccinium*
SPECIES *macrocarpon*

CRANBERRY

Though several species of cranberry are grown commercially, by far the most common is *macrocarpon*. Cranberries grow in several states and Canadian provinces, but Wisconsin produces more than half of all the berries grown in the United States. Massachusetts and New Jersey also grow a considerable amount, but they can't compete with the available land and soil quality typically found in the bogs located in the central and northern areas of the Badger State. Moreover, the Wisconsin bogs are, for the most part, newer and bigger, with wider dikes and more efficient irrigation systems. This makes growing, pollinating, managing, and harvesting the berries more efficient and economical.

Cranberries were a food of the early Native Americans, who shared them with the colonists, it is said, at the first Thanksgiving, which is the time of year they are harvested. For decades, Native Americans were involved with production and harvest of the crop in the leading states, especially Wisconsin. The berries, in a variety of forms, are still popular holiday fare, though cranberries have expanded their popularity in hundreds of different uses.

Like all members of the Ericaceae family, cranberries crave an acidic soil, but unlike other members, they require a well-drained bed. The short, woody vines bloom in early summer, and growers arrange to have at least one colony, sometimes as many as three, per acre of bog brought in to pollinate the small, well-hidden blossoms. Because bogs are usually surrounded by forests, there is often little else for bees to forage on, and, though cranberry blossoms aren't generous with nectar, a small crop of honey is sometimes made. Occasionally, little nectar or pollen is harvested because of poor flying weather and overpopulation, and colonies may actually weaken during pollination.

Growers saturate bogs with bees to make sure that as many flowers as possible get visited and set fruit. (The USDA estimates 20 million blossoms per acre of bog.) The upward re-curved flower petals are light pink, and the reddish reproductive parts inside are longer than the petals and hang exposed. A foraging bee must hang upside down to reach to the bottom of the flower for the very tiny bit of nectar produced. In so doing, she brushes, and sometimes intentionally vibrates, the anthers to get the protein-rich pollen to fall down the pipelike opening and catch on her hairy underside. When the bee travels to another flower to gather nectar, her pollen-covered belly brushes the next flower's sticky stigma, which is longer than the anthers, and pollen transfer occurs. Though a cranberry blossom can pollinate itself, because of its anatomy, it essentially never does and needs insects for pollen transfer.

The fruit, as you are probably aware, is ruby red when ripe, and dark pink inside. It is crisp to bite and at once sweet, sour, and bitter. Berries are seldom eaten raw. A term often used for the flavor of raw cranberries is "severely tart."

As a result of the high population of bees in a bog—which offers excellent pollination of the many flowers but reduces the available nectar to each colony to nearly zero—along with uncertain weather, cranberry honey is erratically produced in small quantities, even in well-managed bogs by good beekeepers. Finding cranberry honey can be a task, and finding it very long after it is harvested is uncommon, even in the locations where it is produced.

CRANBERRY HONEY TASTING NOTES

FRUIT
WARM
WOODY

From the unmistakable deep red color to its red berry tart flavor, every aspect of cranberry honey is reminiscent of the cranberry fruit. If you are lucky enough to get your hands on a jar, do not wait until Thanksgiving to indulge. Although the aroma is slightly pungent, with undercurrents of warm sour milk and tea, cranberry honey is buttery on the tongue, and its flavor oozes tart red cranberries, warm cinnamon spice, and candied fruit. Underneath is a hint of brown sugar and dried plums. It's a lip smacker.

Cranberry honey drizzled over brie that has been baked with whole cranberries and pecans makes a classic presentation. Sip some orange-flavored Grand Marnier to make the occasion celebratory. Cranberry honey is a perfect complement to all your favorite holiday dishes. Glaze your Thanksgiving ham with it. Drizzle it over acorn or butternut squash soups or spread it on pumpkin or spice bread.

FIREWEED

FAMILY *Onagraceae*

GENUS *Epilobium,* or now, *Chamaenerion*

SPECIES *angustifolium*

OTHER NAMES willow herb, giant willow herb

Fireweed earns its name because it is the first green to appear after a forest burns, dies, and leaves an opening to the sky. It takes a winter's time for the soil to cool, but come spring, the ground is littered with fireweed seedlings. The tiny seeds have been there, sometimes for years, waiting for the sun to finally shine, offering them a chance to grow and thrive. Given a choice, fireweed favors slightly acidic soil that's just a tad damp much of the time, but it will do just fine in dry, gravelly, neutral soil.

Fireweed is a colonizer by nature, a pioneer at heart. It grasps every chance it's given to grow when the sun-grabbing clutter of the tall and mighty have fallen. When railroads opened vast stretches of once wooded land, fireweed followed in their wake. New roads and open fields, avalanche shear, and even newly made shallow-river sandbars are all opportune spaces for fireweed to grow. In fact, it used to be known as bombweed, because it grew rapidly in the disturbed soil of craters from the bombs dropped in Europe during World War II.

Apart from needing light, fireweed will grow anywhere that's not desert or covered with ice. The earth's entire Northern Hemisphere is home to this three- to nine-foot, single-stemmed perennial, but it loves the northern United States, especially the

Pacific Northwest and Alaska, as well as Canada. It spreads rapidly —a single plant produces sixty to eighty thousand seeds every year—and spreads rhizomes from its roots to form dense clusters of magenta pink flowers when it blooms in the summer.

Flowers start in June and show off all the way to September. The flowers first appear halfway up the plant, and it takes all summer for blossoms to climb to the top. A beekeeper seeking fireweed honey has a big window for the bees to gather nectar from the many clusters. In fact, beekeepers move their bees from lower altitudes, from fields of clover, from almost anywhere, to a fireweed stand if there's fireweed to be had. Because fireweed is the first to grow in wounded locations, no other flowers or nectar is available there, so it's easy to make pure fireweed honey.

After pollination occurs, assisted greatly by honey bee visitation, thousands of seeds are set, and the flowers fade and fall away as new flowers attract those same honey bees. The seeds gradually mature, held safe and secure in a long pod-like capsule. Each tiny seed has a tuft of fluff attached, and when it's time, the pod splits open and the tufted seeds are blown away. The spread and lift of that tuft is greatly affected by the level of humidity, as dry air causes the tuft to spread its wings and travel on to damper places, where it has the best chance to grow, while humid air causes it to rapidly plummet to the moist earth, where it also likes to be.

In Alaska fireweed is famous, and those who know, know that those first-to-bloom blossoms are also the first to send out seeds; just as the top flowers begin to show is when those thousands of seeds below begin to be released. Clustered together, those thousands of tufts resemble cotton. "When the fireweed starts to cotton, winter is only six weeks away," goes the local wisdom.

When the forest returns, naturally after a burn or planted by man after logging opens the sky, fireweed can't compete. The shade from taller plants spells the end of its run, and after only a very few years the fields and the forest floor no longer sing pink in the spring. Only the seeds remain, waiting again for the sky to open and the sun to shine on another generation of fireweed flowers.

FIREWEED HONEY TASTING NOTES

WARM FRUIT CHEMICAL

How can you not think about smoke and heat when you hear the name fireweed honey? Don't be alarmed, though, because you will not find either of those qualities when you smell or taste this varietal. Fireweed honey is crystal clear, pale straw yellow, with sunny hues of butterscotch and sunflower. It isn't necessary to dip your nose very deep into the jar to be greeted by the warm aromas of brown sugar and dried fruit mingling with subtle hints of curdled milk and yeast. Its texture is pure velvet on your tongue, with a consistency reminiscent of jam. As it melts, you'll sense flavors of poached pears, dried pineapple, and slight caramel notes that quickly fade, leaving a brown sugar aftertaste. There's a slight metallic note in fireweed honey, but it doesn't stick around long. The flavors are richly layered and sweet.

Fireweed honey is a perfect match with Gorgonzola cheese rolled in pistachios with a dry Moscato d'Asti. Drizzle this honey over sweet potatoes or carrots. Use it to top rich vanilla bean ice cream, ginger snaps, or cinnamon and raisin teacakes.

GALLBERRY

FAMILY *Aquifoliaceae*

GENUS *Ilex* (the hollies)

SPECIES *glabra*

OTHER NAMES inkberry, Appalachian tea, evergreen winterberry

Almost every species in the *Ilex* genus is a good honey plant, producing marketable quantities of attractive, flavorful honey. They are unaffected with serious problems from errant weather, environmental upheavals, or attempts by humans to get rid of them because, though native, they can be invasive, troublesome, and dangerous.

So much gallberry grows that it simply dominates the scene. Most of the rest of the hollies are more ornamentals than wild plants, but if you happen to run across a varietal honey made from any of the hollies, make it a point to get some; they're all enticing.

Despite aggressive development in many of the places gallberry naturally occurs, there are still ample acres of this five-foot, native perennial evergreen shrub. That's because it is fond of wetlands. It likes its feet wet all the time, and it likes acidic soil in areas with three to five feet of rain a year. It tolerates salt, fire, some shade, and even cold. It develops extensive tuberous rhizomatous crowns in dense, multiple-stem stands that enable it to spread and recover from fires.

It's found on salt flats and thrives as an understory in pine flatlands and along the coastal plains of the eastern and southeastern United States, from New Jersey, Delaware, and Maryland, south through the Carolinas, extensively in Georgia and Florida, and west along the gulf to eastern Texas. There are wetland stands in parts of Pennsylvania, Arkansas, and a few other locations, and it is occasionally found farther north. But the damp, hot, humid Southeast is where it grows best.

Unfortunately, development has diminished once bountiful stands, especially in southeast Virginia, North Carolina, and even parts of Georgia. Florida, especially, has seen development encroach on once huge stands, but it still holds fast to thousands of acres along rivers and streams and coastal areas, mixed with tupelo and black titi, and thriving in extremely inhospitable areas. It is aggressive and moves into disturbed areas rapidly, so even though it is being destroyed in some places, it continues to spread to new locales.

Gallberry flowers from early May into June, depending on location, and, like all hollies, its female and male flowers grow on separate plants, so they require insects for pollination. When in bloom, each plant is covered with thousands of small, somewhat showy white flowers. Female flowers are singly produced in leaf axils, producing no pollen but sporting a large pistil in the center of the flower, moist and fragrant with nectar. The male plants are loaded with pollen-filled anthers, which shed early in the morning. Visiting bees start with the pollen flowers, which have some nectar, then move to the female nectar producers, and spread pollen all over the large, sticky pistil, completing both pollination and nectar collection.

The small, quarter-inch-long dark blue fruit—a drupe, actually, like a cherry, peach, or olive—is ripe by late summer and, though bitter (as are the leaves and other plant parts, which can be somewhat toxic), serve as wildlife food that will hang on all winter, hence one of its common names. The berries contain caffeine-like compounds and can be used to make a tea.

Before development began disturbing some of the huge stands, there were thousands and thousands of acres of gallberry in the Southeast, and beekeepers were able to consistently make abundant, profitable crops from the plant every year, no matter how many colonies they put in a location. So desired was the honey, however, that it seldom made it out of the region where it was produced, not unlike sourwood and some others even today. To discourage northern beekeepers from moving south to take advantage of this crop, southern beekeepers spread scary and exaggerated stories of the hardships of moving to and staying in gallberry territory.

One report, published in *Gleanings in Bee Culture*, the national beekeeping trade magazine, put it like this: "There are venomous snakes, mosquitoes and red bugs galore. The population is sparse, the villages are small and primitive and the roads are poor. Winters and springs are damp and chilly, the summers extremely hot, and there are few modern conveniences."

The stories must have worked, as you still will seldom find gallberry honey outside the southeastern United States, which hoards so many fine honeys.

GALLBERRY HONEY TASTING NOTES:

Gallberry honey is a richly textured and flavored honey that rarely leaves the state or makes it to a jar; most of this honey is sold to the baking industry for breads, cakes, and cookies. Many people outside of Georgia have never heard of it, yet Slow Food's International Ark of Taste has named gallberry honey one of our planet's endangered foods. Gallberry honey has a deep crimson red color that is almost opaque. You'll be charmed by its gentle aroma,

FRUIT
WOODY
FRESH

which is slightly fruity and mildly acidic. This luscious, heavy-bodied honey coats the tongue like a blanket and imparts flavors of dried fruit, jammy mangos, apricots, and red berries that balance with remote notes of balsamic and pine. Full of pollen, gallberry honey sits in the back of your throat and just might make you cough. This is one honey that is richly flavored but not overpowering.

Gallberry honey pairs well with a citrusy Boucheron goat cheese and chardonnay. Drizzle it over warm corn bread, crispy southern fried chicken, and sautéed, buttered carrots.

Goldenrod has a rich history in American beekeeping because it is both common and abundant in the northeastern United States, where beekeeping first took hold in this country. It produces predictably large honey crops at a time of year when most other stable crops—including alfalfa, all of the clovers, any of the trees, and, of course, the many spring and summer nectar sources—have long gone, so it is valued by both bees and beekeepers as a reliable source of winter honey. Only the asters are left when goldenrod blooms, and aster honey is not even close to being a prime crop.

Although common in the Northeast and sparse in the Deep South, species of goldenrod are found across the United States and in most of Canada; even Mexico has some species. Few natural goldenrods are found in Europe, but many more have been imported there from the United States and are used as garden ornamentals. Certainly, the various environments where goldenrod is found are radically different, but the varieties that have adapted themselves to these very different locales, though similar when it comes to appearance, are not the same in their production of nectar and pollen.

GOLDENROD

FAMILY *Asteraceae*
GENUS *Solidago*
SPECIES more than one hundred

Goldenrod is a perennial, usually with a single stalk and flower head. It spreads using both seeds and rhizomes branching out from the roots. Once a plant is established from seed, the rhizomes will produce a strong, dense stand of identical plants, sometimes covering hundreds of square feet in a field. Goldenrod occupies a variety of habitats, ranging from damp and swampy to high and dry. Shady locations are usually not productive, while full sun is definitely an advantage. Therefore, goldenrod is often found on the sides of roads, at the

edges of fields and fences, and in unused and abandoned fields. Depending on the variety, moisture requirements range from damp to dry, but blossoming for most varieties requires dry weather and moderate soil moisture. The blossoms range in color from cream to striking golden yellow and vary from small, compact, and barely noticeable to spiky plumes that rise far above the topmost leaves, as well as huge, drooping plumes. Each blossom is composed of hundreds of small florets, each offering an abundance of nectar and pollen.

Goldenrod varieties vary from a barely visible two inches tall to almost four feet in height. A compact stand of stout, stalked plants huddled close and all rhizome related could be a formidable obstacle to pass through, allowing it to remain protected from omnivores or other potentially destructive pests. And because such a stand dominates its environment, it becomes a monoculture of sorts, attracting hordes of various consumers—honey bees for nectar and pollen, locust beetles for pollen, butterflies and moths for the nectar, and many other pollinators that depend on the resources these plants provide. And along with the consumers come their predators. In the northeastern United States, there are often as many praying mantis adults among the flowers as there are bees and butterflies.

One rather odd thing occurs when honey bees make goldenrod honey. When goldenrod is abundant and the weather is hot and sunny, the plants produce an incredible amount of nectar and pollen, and bees works feverishly to gather as much as possible and bring it back to the hive, where it is stored. As the bees work to dehydrate that nectar, a by-product is released that is unique to this honey and that carries with it an unmistakable and highly yeasty aroma that has been described—depending on who you ask—as of gym socks or a musty beer. Beginning beekeepers are often alarmed by the odor because it fills an entire bee yard,

making the whole area smell highly unpleasant. When the aroma eventually disappears, what stays behind is an outstanding varietal honey, one worth searching for.

GOLDENROD HONEY TASTING NOTES

FLORAL
VEGETAL
WOODY

Goldenrod honey is perfectly transparent when extracted from the hive, flashing a radiant buttery gold to a luminous dusty orange. That is until it rapidly crystallizes into a thick paste inside the jar. So indulge quickly, because this honey feels downright hedonistically silky on your tongue. You'll want to savor its bright, passionate flavors of peony and honeysuckle as they dance on your palate and then envelop your entire mouth. Goldenrod is intensely animated and beautifully balanced. The experience ends with warm spicy notes that may remind you that autumn is creeping near. As you swallow, prepare for that familiar back-of-the-throat burn.

A few species of goldenrod, more midwestern than northeastern, produce a honey that more resembles butterscotch than honey. It doesn't crystallize as rapidly as other varieties and remains smooth, full bodied, and almost too sweet, if that's possible. Like many other honeys, this localized variety seldom escapes its neighborhood and is rabidly sought after by the local population. Good luck finding it, but if you do, get all you can. You won't be disappointed.

Pair this honey with a crumbly, nutty Manchego or Piave cheese and a sparkling Riesling. Add it to a raw ginger, beet, and carrot smoothie. Goldenrod honey is much sought after by mead makers because of the depth of flavor it adds to the brew.

KUDZU

Kudzu is the most aggressive, destructive, invasive plant covered in this book. And that's saying a lot considering some of the other plants we've examined. The millions of acres it has occupied, the buildings it has pulled down, the utility infrastructure it has destroyed, the thousands of trees it has killed are almost beyond imagination. It truly is "the vine that ate the South."

This perennial is a native of Southeast Asia and is common in China, Japan, and Korea; the name *kudzu* is a mispronunciation of the Japanese name for the plant, *kuzu*. It was brought to this country in 1876, to

FAMILY *Fabaceae*

GENUS *Pueraria*

SPECIES *montana*

OTHER NAMES kudzu vine, foot-a-nite vine, vine that ate the South

Philadelphia to help with Pennsylvania's erosion problems, and in 1883 it was introduced to the South as an ornamental for shading porches. By 1900 it was also being sold by mail order as a source of high-protein cattle feed.

By 1946 the U.S. Soil Erosion Service had distributed 85 million seedlings, which were planted on more than three million acres. By 1953 the Soil Erosion Service had seen the error of its ways and declared kudzu a weed. It was too late.

Kudzu has spread to the point where eradication is no longer viable; merely containing it is an expensive and difficult battle. With a $6 million per year (basically unsuccessful) containment cost, kudzu continues to spread to about 150,000 new acres every year and has no sign of stopping. It has conquered thirty-one states—from southern New York to East Texas and every state east and south of that line. Plus, it has roots in Hawaii, Washington, and Oregon. It now covers about twelve thousand square miles, an area about the same size as Connecticut, Rhode Island, and Delaware combined, or the bottom third of Indiana.

Like all legumes kudzu fixes nitrogen in the soil, enriching it for its own use, and grows on nearly any kind of soil. Seeds, or more commonly rooting nodes on the stem, facilitate reproduction; and, though seedlings aren't terribly competitive with native plants, once established, they completely dominate the space they are in. When a node forms roots, they grow at least nine feet deep and eventually become huge and starchy, holding water for drier times. Because there is no woody stem as such, the plant puts a great deal of energy and growth into the roots; as much as 40 percent of a single plant's biomass is below the surface of the soil. As they mature, the roots form a crown that sends out thirty or more shoots each season. When you figure thirty or more hundred-foot vines on a single plant in a season, the root system supporting that growth is more than impressive.

As the plant grows, twining tendrils form at leaf nodes, enabling the vines to attach and climb almost any object to almost any height. The weight of the vines has pulled down buildings, power poles, and utility lines. They climb trees, pulling off the limbs and leaving only the main trunk. The foot-wide leaves will smother, shade, and obliterate any plant in the way. Or they'll root at a node on the soil surface and start another plant. In northern regions with regular frosts, plants die back to the crown but sprout again in April or May. The following warning comes from a weed control specialist in South Carolina: "Since this weed is an adaptable, aggressive competitor that can rapidly overgrow native vegetation, the presence of any kudzu should trigger control activities. *There is no acceptable population level.*"

Bloom begins in June in the far South and as late as early August in the North, continuing until September or October. Flower spikes at leaf nodes are six inches to a foot long, with red to magenta or, rarely, white flowers, beginning to bloom at the base of the spike and moving up as the season progresses. Self-fertile, they form two- to three-inch seed pods.

The flowers are extremely fragrant. They are a typical legume blossom, with a large red or magenta standard petal on top and a bright yellow nectary guide on the bottom in the center of the flower. There's a wing petal on each side and a keel petal in the center that covers the pistil and stamens. Early in the bloom season the flower spikes are shy and seldom seen above the foliage; as summer moves on, they become so numerous that they are easily seen. The fragrant and sweet-tasting blossoms are used to make a grape-tasting jelly, tastier than real grape jelly, say many folks.

The honey that's produced when there's adequate rain, not too much warmth, and enough bees to visit is absolutely unique.

It is as red as a glass of grape juice, and it tastes like grape juice. Some say it has more of a bubble gum flavor, but either way, there's nothing else like it.

FRUIT FLORAL

Kudzu honey is affectionately known as the purple-colored honey. When the light hits it from the side, you get a glimpse of its flame red highlights. It resembles grape juice, and beekeepers can see the deep purple hue even when kudzu is still in the comb. The aroma is bold, fragrant, and fruity, sometimes described as a cross between Jolly Rancher candy and pink bubble gum. Kudzu is a runny honey with a low viscosity and will pour more easily than most. Once it is on the tongue, grape jelly lovers will enjoy the opulent blackberry and grapey notes that mingle with those of fruity cooked apple and peach. There's a hint of floral jasmine underneath the prominent grape flavor.

Kudzu is a novelty honey for those who are intrigued by unusual food experiences. Traditional regional recipes include kudzu blossom jelly and kudzu lemonade and tofu with kudzu honey sauce. Drizzle your kudzu honey over grapefruit salad, peach tarts, and pork tenderloin. Enjoy it with a Belgium ale.

LINDEN

FAMILY *Malvaceae*

GENUS *Tilia*

SPECIES *americana*
(American basswood),
cordata (littleleaf linden)

OTHER NAMES basswood,
lime, white basswood,
little-leaf linden

There are essentially two species of lindens common in this country now. The American linden commonly called basswood is native to the east, excluding southern Florida and the Gulf Coast regions. The little-leaf linden, which is a European introduction used almost exclusively as a street tree in many cities and towns, covers an even broader region than its native cousin.

The American linden is an excellent timber tree and does well as a pyramid-shaped specimen tree in a large, open setting, but it is most often found in mixed hardwood stands. It will grow to eighty feet tall and spreads out half that in width. It is an imposing tree, growing best in sandy loams, loams, and silt loams that are well drained with a limestone base. River bottoms are a favorite. Soil acidity can range from very acidic to slightly basic, and the tree will even grow, though slowly, on stony, poor, dry locations. Its thin bark and shallow roots make it a victim in fires, but it does send up numerous secondary trees from its shallow roots, if nutrition and sunlight are adequate, eventually producing stands of trees in a close location. Speaking of nutrition, the linden's roots are built to absorb and bring to the tree's leaves significant amounts of calcium and magnesium from deep below the surface of the earth. It then makes those elements available to its roots again, as well as to those of other plants, by discarding its leaf litter. Along with those two elements,

good amounts of nitrogen, phosphorus, and potassium are brought up the same way, helping everything nearby to grow.

The American linden does not make as good a street tree as the little-leaf linden for two reasons. Reflected heat from concrete surfaces can do extensive damage to American lindens by shortening their useful lives and causing premature leaf drop and branch dieback. Lindens are also particularly susceptible to several sap-sucking pests, especially aphids. When trees are heavily infested, which isn't uncommon, the aphids produce a waste product from the sap they are sucking in such quantities that it drips and runs off the leaves and falls to the sidewalk below, or all over a car parked underneath. The sap is sticky, attracts other insects, supports black mold growth, and can damage the finish on a car. It is an

untidy mess and can last much of the summer. To treat the tree is not really feasible, unless you hire a professional. Spraying the aphids with some sort of pesticide to cover an eighty-foot-tall, forty–foot-wide tree with a two-gallon home sprayer is laughable. Hence, American lindens are not favored as shade trees.

The little-leaf linden, by contrast, enjoys the extra heat and reflected light from streets and sidewalks, thrives in poor urban soils, and is practically immune to our pests and predators. Plus, its much smaller leaves mean a much reduced leaf litter problem come autumn. You couldn't ask for much more from a street tree.

Linden blossoms, appearing May to July, depending on how far north they are, are whitish yellow and grow in groups of six to twenty, hanging downward. They are wonderfully fragrant and dripping with nectar, most years. They are attached to a bract two to five inches long that, when the seeds ripen in late summer, acts as sort of a parachute and aids in seed dispersal away from the parent tree.

If the weather cooperates, a linden tree offers anywhere from 100 to 200 pounds of honey—not nectar, honey—in its short season. However, apart from the weather, several things can, and often do, go wrong with lindens, bees, and honey production. First, lindens produce all that nectar on a somewhat random basis, three years out of five being the average for good nectar production. Second, those millions of quarter- to half-inch blossoms are extremely sensitive to heat and low humidity, and in most places bloom time and summer time coincide. Hot, dry winds will dry up those fragile blossoms in a heartbeat, and any nectar produced simply vanishes, leaving nothing behind for our honey bees to harvest.

When conditions are ideal, though, lindens are prolific honey-producing trees. Because so many towns and cities now use little-leaf lindens as street trees, the pos-sibility of above-average honey harvests for urban beekeepers is promising. If one tree can produce one hundred pounds of honey, think what a thousand blocks of those trees could produce for a city beekeeper. The prospects are certainly encouraging, which is fantastic, because not nearly enough basswood honey is produced.

LINDEN HONEY TASTING NOTES

GREEN HERBAL FRUIT EARTHY

If tulip poplar honey is the port of honeys, then linden is the chardonnay. It is delicate, fruity, and sophisticated. Pure linden honey beams a somewhat transparent butter yellow to a golden harvest color. Dip your nose into a jar of linden, and you'll be greeted by subtle hints of sour milk, beeswax, and a sweet mustiness. Linden honey has variegated flavors that are young and gentle and include a hint of green bananas and kiwi. The main attraction, though, is more a gush of butterscotch and pineapple with overtones of crispy green melon. Depending upon where it's harvested you may notice a metallic aftertaste. The flavors fade prematurely, giving linden an exceptionally short finish, which may make you feel that it has teased you and then left you flat. Not entirely, though. This fine honey enhances so many foods that you'll forgive the abrupt ending.

Linden honeys pair well with a creamy, rustic Swiss tomme vaudoise cheese, as well as a buttery Camembert or a New York State Sprout Creek Farm Ouray. Perfect accompaniments are green grapes, toasted pecans, and a crusty baguette. Wash it down with a glass of—what else?—chardonnay. Drizzle linden over a freshly sliced green tomato and honeydew salad with cilantro, or seared scallops and poached pears with sprigs of spearmint.

ORANGE BLOSSOM

AND OTHER CITRUS

FAMILY *Rutaceae*

GENUS *Citrus*

SPECIES *sinesis* (sweet orange), *reticulata* (mandarin), *paradise* (grapefruit), *limon* (lemon), *aurantifolia* (lime), *clementina* (clementine)

Citrus trees—oranges, in particular—have been under cultivation since about 2500 BC and remain the most common fruit tree in the world. Early explorers brought sour orange citrus to Europe from Asia, and it was common there by the mid-1600s. Sweet oranges, common today, also came to Europe from Asia, via Spanish explorers to South America, and finally came to Florida by the 1870s. Once in North America, sweet oranges were grafted onto sour orange rootstock and migrated to Arizona and California.

Citrus are semitropical shiny-leaved evergreens, many with formidable thorns. Extremely sensitive to cold, they can be killed if the temperature falls below 20°F, so they are usually found in the warmest of climates. Most bloom in the spring, though some varieties have blooms that linger into summer, and lemons and limes bloom all year. Flowers remain open until fruit is set, and the fruit, once ripe, can remain on the tree without deteriorating. It is common to see a tree blooming while still holding last season's crop.

The extremely fragrant blossoms range from three-quarters to one and a half inch across, appearing all at the same time in a grove, and are loaded with nectar. Typically, each blossom has about twenty microliters of nectar, compared to a burgeoning alfalfa blossom, which has maybe two microliters. A single bee cannot harvest all of the nectar in a blossom, and seldom are there enough bees to take advantage of all the nectar available in a grove. Nectar flow is so abundant that fruit pickers often end their day soaked with the fragrant, sugary liquid. Nectar production begins midmorning, peaks at around noon, when the rather poor-quality pollen is released, and slows to very little at around four p.m.

Almost all varieties of citrus are self-fertile, and insect pollination isn't required for fruit production, but exchanging pollen between similar varieties may increase seed production. This can marginally increase fruit size but may be detrimental for quality.

Florida produces about 70 percent of the U.S. citrus crop, with about 541,000 acres of mostly juice oranges, grapefruit, clementines, tangerines, tangelos, blood oranges, lemons, limes, and a few others. For perspective, there are about 25 million orange trees in Florida, producing nearly 15 billion pounds of oranges, and squeezing out over 80 million gallons of orange juice.

California's production is a distant second, with only 180,000 acres of mostly eating oranges, but also of lemons and other citrus crops. Total production is only 5 billion pounds of fruit. Texas and Arizona also produce citrus, but they are a distant third compared to the two big producers, their combined total just short of a billion pounds of all citrus grown.

Florida produces only half of what Brazil produces annually; between the two, they own 85 percent of the world's orange market. Orange honey, it's easy to see, comes from not a lot of places, but those few places produce a lot of it.

Although orange blossom honey comes from oranges, some percent of grapefruit is almost always mixed in, along with smaller amounts of tangerine, tangelo, lemon, and lime. Pure grapefruit honey is interesting because like a few other rare honeys, it is extremely thixotropic, which means that, as it is extracted and bottled, it sets up as a gel. Sometimes it even sets up in the hive,

before the beekeeper can remove it. It can't be poured out of a jar or squeezed out of a bear. If shaken it returns to a liquid, just like the rest of the citrus honeys examined here, and it's just as sweet and just as fragrant.

ORANGE BLOSSOM HONEY TASTING NOTES

FRUIT

FLORAL

WARM

Orange blossom honey is every bit as sweet as a freshly squeezed glass of orange juice. The color is a medium amber, as golden as the sun that helped the fruit to grow and that glows with hues of burnt orange and a fiery tangerine. A whiff of orange blossom honey is like a stroll through the Florida orange groves in full bloom. Highly aromatic notes of hyacinth and honeysuckle combine with the citrus. The rapture continues on your tongue with crisp, vibrant notes of orange and tangerine lollipops that harmonize with bouquets of jasmine perfume. Relatively light bodied, round, and feminine, this honey is a real mouth pleaser.

If the orange honey hails from Southern California, Arizona, or another desert region, you can expect the color to be much darker, in the dusty amber family, with a butterscotch tint. Orange blossom from the desert reflects its terroir—you taste the warm, sandy desert in every spoonful. The citrus flavors are earthier and somewhat maple.

This honey is an excellent candidate for infusing with cinnamon, ginger, or rose petals. Orange honey is just waiting to become a honey butter spread, which tastes delicious melted on cranberry-walnut bread. It makes a perfect orange glaze to finish ham, pork, or fried chicken and goes just as well in desserts. Try drizzling it over a pistachio and chocolate ganache tart.

PURPLE LOOSESTRIFE

There's a wealth of information available about the purple loosestrife plant, much of it well researched by government agencies trying to figure out how to make it go away. Purple loosestrife was introduced to the US in the 1800s from the United Kingdom and brought here as an ornamental. It was abundant in the UK, throughout central and southern Europe, east to Russia and Japan, and south to Southeast Asia and India. North America was one of the few places it hadn't already colonized. It doesn't do well in extreme cold or heat, so the temperate belt of the globe is where it thrives.

FAMILY *Lythraceae*
GENUS *Lythrum*
SPECIES *salicaria*
OTHER NAMES *purple lythrum*

Purple loosestrife is a four- to ten-foot-tall herbaceous perennial, and when mature it produces thirty to fifty magenta to pink flowering spikes that show from July to October. It likes wet feet. It thrives in natural and especially in disturbed wetlands as a pioneer and likes freshwater wet meadows, tidal and nontidal marshes. It shows up along river and stream banks and pond edges, in damp ditches, along roadsides, and even in cranberry bogs. It does well in damp, wet, or standing water locations. It favors slightly acid to neutral soil but does fine in slightly basic and infertile soils, too. When submerged in water, the roots and crown grow special cells that transfer air to the growing tips.

Purple loosestrife, since it arrived, has aggressively occupied wet places in almost every state except in the desert Southwest and tropical Southeast. Because initially it had no natural enemies, it spread slowly but unhindered. When it moves in, it gradually replaces cattails, grasses, sedges, and other native aquatic plants, some endangered. It also colonizes areas where other plants don't grow, primarily in shallow open-water areas. This has challenged habitat and food resources for some wildlife in those places, but not quite as much as was first thought.

Purple loosestrife wasn't considered a problem until the 1950s, because its spread was moderate and its effect was not considered detrimental. Eventually, the insidiousness of its advance became obvious. Those thirty to fifty flowering spikes, each with hundreds of individual flowers, can produce up to three million seeds every year. Each of those hundreds of flowers must be fertilized with a similar flower from another plant (loosestrife has three kinds of flowers, similar but of different sizes). Honey bees are both essential and efficient in helping to spread this plant. It is suspected that beekeepers have offered some assistance, too.

As the plants mature, they form a large crown just beneath the surface of the soil, or water, from which those flowering spikes arise. They also have a deep taproot, which does just fine when water levels shrink, and large, lateral side roots that both supply water to the original plant and produce additional plants. Together these roots and the crown will form a dense stand about twenty inches in diameter, all genetically identical, and thick enough to stop a boat—or the water flow in a creek or swamp. When the plants are thick enough, and have been in one place long enough (stands more than twenty years old are not uncommon), the geography of a streambed is changed, wildlife and native plants are left dry or flooded, and ponds form or are drained. Purple loosestrife is a dynamic game changer in its chosen environment.

Conquering new territory isn't all that difficult. With the millions of seeds produced, and the many mature plant stands that appear in a location over time, it isn't uncommon to have thirty to forty thousand loosestrife seeds per square foot in the top two inches of soil, simply waiting to germinate. The rest, of course, simply float downstream, or across the pond or wetland, or are picked up by animals or humans and moved to another location. Mowing is not even an effective removal technique, because the cut pieces of stem can root right where they fall. Determined forces have decided that the spread of this beautiful but troublesome plant must be contained and even reduced. Scientists have imported to the U.S. several leaf- and root-feeding beetles from its original home in Eurasia that are slowly overcoming the advance of this weed.

Loosestrife is similar in appearance to several native plants, including fireweed, blue vervain, and liatris, but a key in identifying this plant is that it has square, or even five- or six-sided stems, where the others' stems are typically round.

One unique aspect of loosestrife honey is that, when first harvested, it has a green tinge to it, sometimes very green. Some say it looks like motor oil, but those who have tasted it know it is even more precious than that expensive liquid.

PURPLE LOOSESTRIFE TASTING NOTES

WARM VEGETAL FRESH

A rare and often unwelcomed honey, purple loosestrife is easily recognized by its extremely dark mineral color and odd green-bluish tint. It is highly aromatic, with medicinal and herbal notes. The flavor is surprisingly delicate and sweet, with notes of tobacco and strong black tea, ending with a tang on the tongue.

Purple loosestrife is strictly labeled a bakery-grade honey; it is blended with other honeys and sold for using in cookies, cakes, and cereals. Mead and honey winemakers are fond of its strong flavors, which give their beverages a distinctive taste.

SAW PALMETTO

FAMILY *Arecaceae*
GENUS *Serenoa* or *Sereno*
SPECIES *repens*
OTHER NAMES *scrub palmetto*

Much like sourwood, mesquite, and fireweed, this restricted-region honey is not produced just any-where, like clover or goldenrod. It is highly favored, and hoarded, in its home region, limiting the supply available for the rest of us. One of the keys to demand is, of course, supply, but, more important, the product must be worthy of the demand. There's no doubt palmetto honey is one of the finest honeys produced.

Saw palmetto is native to Florida, the southernmost tip of Georgia, easing up to the southern tip of South Carolina, then following the Gulf Coast west to just touch eastern Louisiana. But is it is an adaptive species, and it has spread all over the south-eastern part of the United States, partly be-cause it makes an attractive and long-lived ornamental, and partly because it is the most cold hardy of all the palms, surviving in cold as low as 25°F. Below that critical cold temperature it doesn't survive at all.

It does have some soil requirements that limit its range. It strongly favors a dry, well-drained, sandy soil and fares poorly, if at all,

when drainage is limited. It likes full sun to partial shade and does well as understory in oak and pine stands common in that part of the country. It needs four to five feet of rain—yes, feet—each growing season, partly because the soil it grows in holds virtually no water at all, and partly because it transpires quite freely. It is drought tolerant for short periods, however; it simply doesn't grow when it's dry.

Palmetto is most common as a low-grow-ing shrub, two to seven feet tall, especially in scrubland areas. However, in the mari-time hammocks and inner uplands, it can take the form of a tree, reaching twenty to twenty-five feet when mature. But *mature* is a relative term here, as these plants grow very slowly. Some experts estimate that there are specimens in Florida that have reached anywhere from five hundred to nine hundred years of age.

As a shrub they spread into a clump about twenty feet in circumference above surface, while underground stems throw up more plants. (It's the plants sent up from the underground stems that will successfully recolonize an area devastated after a fire.) Individual plants have twenty to twenty-five fan-shaped, palm-like evergreen leaves, each about three feet across and covered with a waxy film. Leaves are most often green, but occasionally a blue-green or an almost silver variety appears and is sought after as an ornamental. It's the sharp spines on the leaf stems that give the plant its name, saw palmetto, by the way.

Palmettos bloom April through July, producing three-foot branched flower spikes from leaf axils. Small, white to light yellow flowers are densely packed on these spikes and are extremely fragrant, attracting a wide variety of insects to feast on the abundant pollen and seemingly gallons of nectar each spike produces. Flowers begin blooming at the base of the spike, taking about a month for all of them to open. When they first open, you can see the huge amount of nectar at the base of the flower. Pollen is released about two hours after the flower opens and is pretty much gone in about twenty-four hours. However, the stigma, which receives the pollen for fertilization, isn't receptive until a day or so later, so insects are required to transfer freshly released pollen to a day-old flower on that spike, another spike on the same plant, or a receptive flower on a completely different plant. All of these scenarios keep the palmetto's genetic diversity at a healthy, productive level.

Honey bees are by far the most efficient pollinators, scrabbling all over the spikes when they are in bloom, testing for nectar, searching for more, and spreading pollen from flower to flower. Once pollinated, palmettos produce a small berry from each flower on each spike, which ripens August through October. The berries are edible, even tasty. They were common in the diets of early Native Americans and still feed bear and deer. There is some medicinal value in a berry extract, and palmettos are cultivated to a degree for that crop, with honey bees brought in to increase fruit set and, fortunately for us, palmetto honey.

SAW PALMETTO HONEY TASTING NOTES

FRUIT
SPICY
WOODY

Saw palmetto is a specialty honey rarely found outside its local region, so you'll most likely have to go to the source to taste it. It would be well worth the trip. Its striking maroon color and medium amber highlights make it a standout. Saw palmetto has a well-rounded bouquet laced with notes of citrus and subdued wood. Thick and full textured, its flavor is a balance of refreshing anise, nutmeg, and dried prunes, with woody overtones. The flavors slowly fade, leaving a smoky molasses note at the end.

Drizzle saw palmetto honey over a wedge of smoked Gouda and herbed bread, with prosciutto. Saw palmetto adds depth of flavor to ham, turkey, and sausage dishes. Spoon it into black tea or use it to perk up freshly squeezed lemonade.

No other honey is surrounded by as much mystery and legend as sourwood. It almost never escapes its native Appalachian homeland but has been named "Best Honey in the World" twice at the international Apimondia International Apiculture Congress. It is one of beekeeping's poorest-kept secrets.

FAMILY *Ericaceae*
GENUS *Oxydendrum*
SPECIES *arboreum*

SOURWOOD

The sourwood plant gets its name from the sour taste of the leaves and small branches. They contain oxalic acid, a naturally occurring compound found in many plants, including rhubarb and wood sorrel. Oxalic acid is also an effective deterrent to varroa mites in beehives when it is vaporized in the hive or diluted and dissolved in sugar syrup and dripped on the bees. Commonly used as wood bleach, it is corrosive and, at full strength, can cause skin damage if touched or respiratory problems if inhaled.

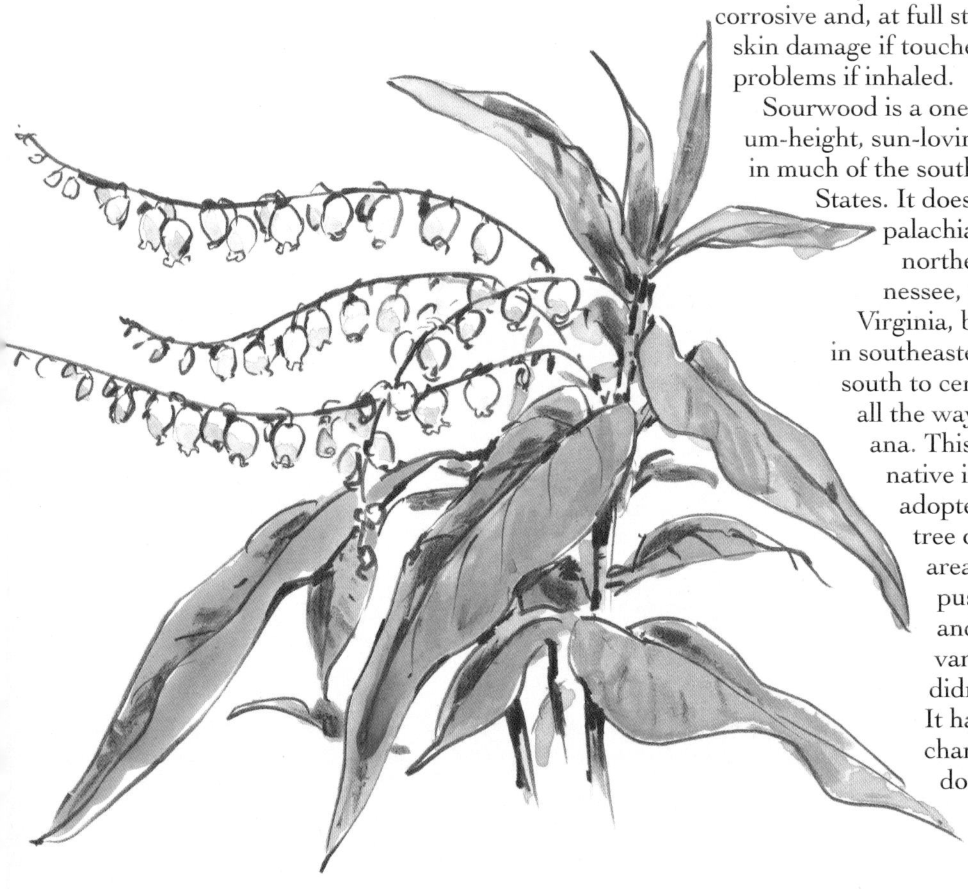

Sourwood is a one-of-a-kind medium-height, sun-loving tree that grows in much of the southeastern United States. It does best in the Appalachian mountains of northern Georgia, Tennessee, the Carolinas, and Virginia, but you can find it in southeastern Pennsylvania, south to central Georgia, and all the way west to Louisiana. This North American native is also now being adopted as a specimen tree outside its native area and has been pushed and pulled and planted in a variety of places it didn't used to inhabit. It has two prime characteristics: It doesn't like winters in the far North, and like all members of the Ericaceae family it needs a strongly acidic soil to thrive. It will, however, grow in less than ideal conditions.

Sourwood is often called the Appalachian lily-of-the-valley tree because of the similarity of its flower's shape and aroma to the fragrant but poisonous shade-loving ground cover of the same name. Sourwood blooms are showy and fragrant, brilliant white contrasting with the rich green of the foliage. They hang in racemes, ripening from the base of the stem toward the end of the flower stalk. Sourwood is related to blueberry, cranberry, rhododendron, heaths, and heathers, all requiring acidic, infertile conditions. When it grows at lower altitudes where the soil is fertile and ample water is available, it may reach fifty feet or more, but as it moves up mountainsides, where soil becomes less fertile and water less common, it stays shorter and is less prolific.

Sourwood blooms late June through early August in its home area, but you have to take those dates with a grain of salt. As you would imagine, the bloom begins in the valleys and lowlands of the Appalachians, but as spring moves up the mountains, the bloom follows, moving all the way into July. In Louisiana bloom doesn't come until September and October. Clever beekeepers follow the bloom to lengthen the time their bees have to collect the exquisite nectar.

Obviously, other trees and shrubs inhabit sourwood's space, and some of them bloom at the same time. Sourwood honey, when it is as pure as you can get it, is crystal clear. Interestingly, it may have an unusual gray cast, but you have to look hard to see it. When a sample is darker than a glass of water, you can bet that other honeys have joined the party. Sumac is a common intruder on sourwood bloom. It's easy to discern, because it is darker and has a more robust flavor. If your sourwood is less than crystal clear, it probably has some sumac honey mixed in, which is not a bad thing,

but it's not sourwood.

Other honeys can also mix in without tarnishing the color of sourwood because they are also as clear as glass. Basswood is a good example. The flavor of basswood is significantly different than sourwood's buttery, creamy, floral experience, and when the two are blended, the result is good but offers the best of neither.

SOURWOOD HONEY TASTING NOTES

WARM VEGETAL FLORAL

Sourwood has been named by Slow Food's Ark of Taste as an endangered honey plant. Pure sourwood honey is a true treasure and deserves its reputation as one of the finest honeys harvested in the United States. The best sourwood honeys are absolutely transparent, with a hint of green. A freshly opened jar smells like the holidays, as warm spicy notes of cinnamon tickle your nose. Sourwood is a sticky honey; the texture is velvety and viscous and prompts one to want to suck or chew it as it sits on the tongue. Sourwood honey often comes with a slice of comb in the jar, which adds a textural dimension to the tasting experience. There is nothing sour about this honey, but rather a complex flavor with notes of anise and cinnamon that explode on the tongue.

Sourwood honey begs to be drizzled over warm gingerbread or cinnamon toast. Try it with sliced figs, blue cheese, and crumbled walnuts. Thanksgiving was made for sourwood honey; add it to sautéed carrots, squash soups, sweet potatoes, and all root vegetables. Use it to sweeten a warm cider rum drink during the cool days of autumn.

STAR THISTLES & KNAPWEEDS

FAMILY *Asteraceae*

GENUS *Centaurea*

SPECIES *maculosa* (generally, knapweed), *solstitalis* (generally, star thistle), and hundreds more

OTHER NAMES yellow or purple star thistle, purple or spotted knapweed

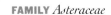

Why is it, do you suppose, that more than half those plants that produce some of the finest honeys seem to be some of the worst invasive weeds? Check out plants we explore here and see for yourself.

Because there are so many species of plants in this genus, we are going to make a somewhat artificial, but to us, logical distinction between these two very broad groups known as star thistles and knapweeds: those plants with yellow flowers are star thistles, and those with purple flowers are knapweeds. Immediately, botanists, honey connoisseurs, ecologists, weed specialists, conservationists, and others will cry foul, because this is, to them, a wrong-headed decision. So be it. For our purposes it works fairly well, and it seems reasonable, considering that we need to distill the information from several hundred species down to the space allotted on these pages. But, more important, to us, at least, is that the honeys produced by all of these species are so very similar, perhaps identical, that separation to a greater degree seems not worth the effort.

Not surprisingly, none of these varieties are indigenous to the United States, having made the trip here from various parts of Europe, North Africa, and Eurasia between the mid-1800s and the early 1900s, mixed in with alfalfa and grass seeds bound for U.S. meadows, grasslands, feedlots, and pastures, or mixed in soil used as ballast in the ships. Ironically, some of these now endemic species in the United States are becoming threatened in their homeland due to urban expansion and agricultural practices.

Though most species were initially introduced in the eastern part of the country and had purple flowers, some began their journey on the West Coast and had yellow flowers. The eastern intruders spread west across much of North America in the ensuing hundred-plus years, mostly thriving in dry, gravelly, recently disturbed soil, reflecting their original environment. Some, however, sought wetter feet and the dry West just wouldn't do. Those have remained mostly in the East or moved westward along river bottomlands. Meanwhile, the western introductions have remained mostly western, not venturing out of the areas where they were first introduced. All species are considered invasive in at least twenty-six states and continue to spread.

Except for flower color most of the species are very similar in appearance—leaves, stems, and flower buds are similar—and habitat, and they can sometimes hybridize within their respective groups, so precise identification can be difficult, except at the genetic level, and even then it's not definitive for some species. The environment required for some to grow well will give away the plant's identity, but most varieties of both colors tend to do well in similar locations, favoring areas that are dry to arid, with low fertility but good drainage and gravelly to sandy soil with neutral to high pH. These include rangelands, pastures, roadsides, and what are often referred to as wastelands. Generally, they bloom from early July to late September, depending on where they are, but almost always beginning before, and lasting longer than, their competitive neighbors.

STAR THISTLE AND KNAPWEED TASTING NOTES

VEGETAL CHEMICAL WOODY

Star thistle and knapweed honeys tend to fall toward the lighter side of amber, often with a greenish cast similar to that of olive oil. When *Centaurea* eventually crystallize, the color transforms into light straw or dark ochre, with attractive yellow to orange hues. Do not let the scent send you running. *Centaurea* has a bold and intense aroma that is chemical and vegetal with animal notes. On the tongue, these honeys are heavily bodied and viscous, delivering a delightful buttery texture. *Centaurea* honey is a mosaic of interesting flavors—you'll find fresh notes of wet grass and green bananas, spicy anise and cinnamon, warm molasses and prunes, with a touch of nutty almonds. Underneath it all are gamy notes that wane quickly into warm caramel.

Centaurea honeys can be paired with an aged Manchego cheese and a glass of Rioja. Drizzle over fried green tomatoes or beignets. Mix it in a vinaigrette to dress an arugula, mango, and pine nut salad, or add it to chamomile tea or, for a unique flavor experience, try a spoonful of warmed starthistle honey.

TAMARISK

FAMILY *Tamaricaceae*

GENUS *Tamarix*

SPECIES *ramosissima* (most common) and several others

COMMON NAMES salt cedar, Athel pine, salt tree

The salt cedars (there are several species) were invited to the West Coast of the United States as ornamental trees from gardens in Eurasia in 1823. They soon proved to be useful windbreaks and shade trees. Depending on species, they range from five to twenty-five feet tall. They have a striking display of up to two-inch-long, dark pink to light pink to white, somewhat fragrant floral spikes made of hundreds of individual florets that form on branch ends from March to September. The salt cedars originally felt right at home in the hot, arid, and uninviting desert, and, for a time, everyone was happy. But it turns out they weren't very nice guests. And, of course, they escaped.

By 1880 salt cedars had colonized Southern California, Arizona, New Mexico, and West Texas and were on the move, crowding out cottonwoods, willows, desert ironwood, and palo verde trees. Today they can be found from Virginia south to Georgia, west to California, and north through the central United States as far as North Dakota. Colonization is easily accomplished because a single large plant produces half a million seeds during the season. If the parent plant is near moving water, the seeds are carried downstream and germinate rapidly in moist soil. Though seedlings are not initially competitive, sheer numbers overwhelm everything growing. And, of course, those seeds were pollinated by honey bees seeking a rich diet of both nectar and pollen from the blossoms.

Salt cedar is at home in established and disturbed streams; on stream banks; in waterways, drainage washes, and irrigation ditches; and almost anywhere water can be found. It rapidly colonizes those locations, producing thick, impenetrable, monocultural stands. It survives extreme heat, freezing, flooding, drought, and burning. In huge stands bird and wildlife diversity vanishes. Its leaves, though small and tight to the stem, fall in the autumn and pile up on the ground or fill waterways to the point of clogging water flow in steams, driving out local fish and native vegetation, even changing the course of rivers and causing flooding in some areas.

The plant needs wet feet because, when it is mature, its almost nonexistent leaves transpire up to two hundred gallons of water a day. Its taproot goes deep, to twenty feet or more to reach the water table, then branches and spreads another fifteen to twenty feet to reach as much water as it can, storing water in all those roots. Salt cedars also have roots on the surface, so they take advantage of standing water, too. A large stand can render ground-water reserves unavailable to other plants and dry out surface water in marshes and springs. Salt cedars are also extremely flammable, so they become excellent fuel for brush fires, which can destroy entire stands, along with every other bit of vegetation in the area. After a fire, the plant is remarkably aggressive, sprouting from the roots and dominating the scene with even denser stands.

The combination of deep roots seeking hard-to-find water and the formation of dense stands led to salt cedar's second exodus. During the 1930s, after years of abusive farming practices and a decade-long drought, the Midwest began to blow away. Wind erosion was removing feet of topsoil, and something was needed as a windbreak, something that could find water in the harshest location. So across the plains, the central United States, and wherever the dustbowl existed, salt cedar

was planted by the government to stop the erosion and stabilize the soil. It dutifully spread beyond the Midwest, of course, and today it has its way to some degree in almost every southern state.

It is the salt in salt cedar that's most intriguing. These plants have the ability to remove naturally occurring salts from deep in the alkaline soils where they thrive and exude them in a crusty, salty layer on their stems. When thousands of these plants colonize a stream bed or meadow, the salt concentration on the soil surface rises dramatically, inhibiting seed germination of almost every native plant. Its own seedlings, of course, don't mind the salt at all, so those millions of seeds have even less competition when they fall.

What is interesting from the perspective of a beekeeper or a honey connoisseur is that the salts a salt cedar removes from the soil in North Dakota are far different than the salts removed from the soils of Arizona, and, though the plants seem to make no distinction, the nectar produced by the flowers, and the plant tissue itself, will reflect that different chemistry. Honey bees favor the blossoms everywhere the plant grows, but because of the salty dining experience, almost nothing else eats salt cedar. It has, at least so far, remained one of the champions of invasive plants.

TAMARISK HONEY TASTING NOTES

WOODY ANIMAL WARM

Salt cedar honey is commonly called tamarisk honey. If you are a fan of dark and savory honeys, this is one to seek out. Tamarisk honey can be recognized by its deep nutmeg color and golden highlights. Its texture is jammy enough to hold your spoon, but it crystallizes rapidly into large unpleasant crystals; when that happens, gently heat the jar until the honey returns to its liquid glory. Expect tame aromas of dark beer and smoky molasses. Tamarisk honey has a thick, felted mouth feel, and it will sit on the tongue for eternity before melting. This is not a sweet honey. You'll find an unusual umami note of soy sauce, with distinct flavors of woody pine and malt and a lingering, smoky, slightly bitter aftertaste.

Tamarisk honey will tame any wedge of stinky blue cheese—try Gorgonzola, Stilton, or Gouda with crumbled hazelnuts and a glass of dark or tawny port. You'll be inspired to light the fireplace. Drizzle it over pulled pork sandwiches, grilled pineapples or papaya. Stir it into black bean soup.

TULIP POPLAR

FAMILY *Magnoliaceae*

GENUS *Liriodendron*

SPECIES *tulipifera*

OTHER NAMES yellow poplar, tulip tree, white poplar, white wood

The tulip poplar tree is one of the most magnificent hardwood trees in the eastern United States. There are only two species of this tree, and the other is in China; so it stands alone in more ways than one. Its natural range is from north central New York south to central Florida, west to the very eastern third of Illinois and Louisiana in the Gulf region. But it thrives best on the Appalachian mountain slopes of North Carolina, Tennessee, Kentucky, and West Virginia. Its favored location is in medium moist, well-drained, loose-textured, loamy soil common to river bottoms and the edges of swamps. The plant has a high nitrogen requirement to thrive, so it's not uncommon to find tulip poplar mixed in with nitrogen-fixing black locust trees. That cohabitation can result in overlapping blooms, and the resulting honey blend, while exquisite, is neither locust nor poplar.

In the northern extreme of their range tulip poplars are seldom found at altitudes higher than 1,000 feet, and even there they stay bundled up in protected valleys and streambed areas. In the southern Appalachian Mountains these trees thrive all the way to 4,500 feet, anywhere they can find the right soil and moisture. The wood of the poplar is straight, white, and easy to work. It was used by Native Americans to make canoes large enough to carry as many as twenty passengers. It is also commonly used for pulp, producing a high-quality paper that needs little whitening, an environmental advantage.

Tulip poplar bloom dates range from April to June, south to north, with the flowers appearing mostly on branches in the upper third of ten-year-old or older trees. People not familiar with these trees seldom even see the blooms until the orange-yellow-green petals begin to fall and litter the ground below. Since older trees are anywhere from 100 to 180 feet tall, 140 feet being the approximate average, it's no wonder the flowers remain unseen. The bloom lasts longest, and produces the most honey, when the early part of the bloom dates are cool and rainy and then the season turns warm and dry.

It's a shame the flowers are so hard to see. They are large, five to seven inches across when open, with six petals that are mostly a soft yellow, but with an orange sherbet splotch on the bottom and a greenish collar just above the orange. A multicolored blossom is uncommon in nature, and this one is striking. Seeds are formed in a cone-shaped array of pistils in the center, surrounded by a ring of pollen-producing anthers. Most of the seeds are infertile, but when honey bees visit the blossoms, the number of seeds increases; if there is a large stand and the flowers are cross-pollinated by honey bees with pollen from another tree, the number of fertile seeds is increased even more. A productive flower will produce a teaspoon of sugar-rich nectar, which drips like rain when the tree is in full bloom. Long ago, beekeepers knew that if a tulip poplar tree was crowded, it produced fewer blooms and thus less honey. Thinning was a regular occurrence in a tulip stand, so the crown of the tree could stretch and grow wide and wild, with hundreds of blooms in the spring.

Reports from the time when there were huge stands of these trees tell that the nectar is composed of over 16 percent sugar when the flower first opens and concentrates it to over 30 percent later on. At this rate, it was reported, a tree could produce over two pounds of honey! The honey is somewhat peculiar. Once cured by the bees and first extracted, it appears to be very dark amber; but when you hold a bottle up to the light, it is definitely a deep, dark red.

TULIP POPLAR HONEY TASTING NOTES

FRUIT FLORAL WARM

Unlike most dark honeys, which have deep and bitter flavors, tulip poplar has approachable notes of sweet caramel and flowers. You will recognize this honey by its deep plum color and the golden highlights visible around the edges as you swirl it around a clear glass. The nose is lively, with vivid bouquets of musty saddle leather and warm caramel mingling with dried fruit. Take note of the syrupy texture, then prepare for a delightfully smooth and buttery mouth feel. The enticing aromas do not stop at your nose. Tulip poplar has flavors that are just as complex and dramatic. At the start, you'll encounter warm sweet notes of raisins, currants, and prunes, then opulent flowers and hints of apples, both of which are curiously savory. All these notes sit on the tongue for what seems like eternity and are just as luscious even as the honey goes down, coating the back of the throat and leaving a cloying honey choke. Tulip poplar honey is somewhat difficult to get ahold of; when you do find it for sale, get yourself three jars of it. You won't be sorry.

Tulip poplar honey pairs well with La Peral, a gently blued, pasteurized cow and sheep milk cheese, or a nutty and buttery Pyrenees Brebis sheep's milk cheese. Drizzle it over baked Brie with freshly sliced apples and walnuts. Tulip poplar honey is reminiscent of a sweet dessert wine, so choose a nice port or vin santo to drink with your cheese and honey pairings. You won't regret pouring tulip poplar over rum raisin or maple walnut ice cream. This summer honey will also add a good flavor to your favorite barbecue sauce, or stir it into a warm pot of spicy baked beans just before serving.

TUPELO

FAMILY *Cornales,* (the dogwood family)

GENUS *Nyssa*

SPECIES *ogeche*

COMMON NAMES white gum, water tupelo, white tupelo

For most beekeepers, when you say "tupelo honey," three things come to mind almost immediately: the 1971 song by Van Morrison; the 1997 movie *Ulee's Gold*, starring Peter Fonda as a beekeeper in Florida; and a nearly perfect honey that's smooth with good body, light color, and mild flavor that never granulates. How much better can it get—music, movies, and the perfect honey?

There are several species in the Nyssa genus of plants. Most are trees or large shrubs, and where they grow greatly influences how large they become. All tend to favor wet feet, and the star of the bunch, white tupelo, lives its whole life in or so close to water that it's wet most of the time. Its wet feet give it great height—one hundred feet or more, and four to five feet in diameter at its maximum. All the tupelos produce honey crops most years—it depends on the water—but it's the white tupelo that is favored by beekeepers.

White tupelo has a limited range, from the very tip of South Carolina, south down the southeastern third of coastal Georgia, and on down to the northern 10 percent or so of Florida all along the Gulf Coast, especially along the north-south rivers of the panhandle. But there's a special region in Florida's panhandle that is the worst-kept secret in the beekeeping world, especially since starring as the setting of the movie *Ulee's Gold*. About fifty miles north of where the Apalachicola River flows into the Gulf of Mexico, it breaks up into a slew of small streams, swamps, stagnant pools, and wetlands. The area is about ten miles wide, and it was, at one time, almost overpopulated with tupelo trees. Beekeepers would migrate to the edges of this area in April and May and situate their colonies on long docks high above the water so their bees could forage out to the trees. Some beekeepers put their hives on boats to carry them to islands in the midst of this vast swamp, hoping that the rainy-season floods were over rather than just beginning. There were, for years, far more trees than the bees could visit, and huge crops of this grand honey could be made every year.

Because it doesn't granulate, tupelo honey was, and still is, highly sought after by northern honey packers and beekeepers. Today, because the area has been logged, somewhat drained, and more or less changed as far as a good place for tupelo to grow, there are only a few beekeepers who take advantage of this marvelous opportunity and harvest this special crop. The docks, at least some of them, still stand above the water, looking across the drying, dying swampland. If you listen close, on a clear, warm spring day, you can just make out some of the lyrics from Van Morrison's song.

TUPELO HONEY TASTING NOTES

WARM FRUIT FLORAL

Tupelo honey has been called the champagne of honeys. It also has been named an endangered honey by Slow Food's Ark of Taste, so prepare to spend a bit more on this highly desirable and world-renowned honey. Tupelo is white or extra light amber, with a greenish cast, it has a pleasant spicy and fruit-filled aroma that invites you right in. Scoop up a big spoonful and prepare for warm notes of cinnamon, butterscotch, and nutmeg, floral jasmine and fruity pears. All these flavors sit on the tongue like smooth butter. Because of its high fructose levels, tupelo is a very sweet-tasting honey and is known to resist crystallization for some time after harvest.

Tupelo pairs nicely with blue cheese, aged Pecorino, Cabrales, and other robust cheeses. Walnuts and Marcona almonds add a nice texture as accompaniments. Enjoy with a glass of champagne or cava. Drizzle it over spicy pears, oatmeal, or ginger pistachio ice cream or add it to spiced pear martinis or chai tea.

Catclaw, guajillo, kiawe, and mesquite honeys have been grouped together not for what they have in common—that they come from desert regions of the southwest United States, Mexico (at least in origin), and parts of South America—but rather, to show the differences in how plants of the same family, and even the same genus, can differ in their requirements of soil, water, and location while growing together. Even so, their outward appearance is similar except for size, with the same leaf structure and rugged, crooked, but dense stems and branches.

The four—catclaw, guajillo (pronounced gwah-HEE-yoh), kiawe (Kee AH vay), and mesquite—are all legumes in the family Fabaceae, home of soybeans, beans, alfalfa, and peas, to name a few. Of course, they have their bad cousins, too, including broom, gorse, and kudzu, all noxious weeds (but good honey producers) that thrive in many parts of the world. Guajillo and catclaw are native to the Southwest, but kiawe (a mesquite cousin) and mesquite are extremely invasive and not native to their new homes: Kiawe moved from South America to Hawaii, and mesquite moved north from Mexico to take over much of what used to be grasslands in the southwestern United States.

You probably couldn't drive a truck through a thicket of these plants because they are so dense and crowded, but then you probably wouldn't be driving where they grow anyway, because they find the deepest, steepest arroyos and river trenches in the region to live in. These six- to twenty-five-foot-tall trees are by far the most drought tolerant of the desert honey plants, and they have adapted to drought conditions in a variety of ways. Of course, growing where they do means that when it does rain, they will get water, and their deep roots continue to tap that resource long after the rains have gone. When it comes, however, the water comes in a rush, and this is important. Catclaw seeds need to be scarified—that is, bruised and beaten—to weaken their very tough seed coat so they can germinate. Simply falling on the ground in a pod isn't enough. There was a time when large omnivores were common in the same regions, and they made daily desserts of this somewhat sweet and,

CATCLAW

FAMILY *Fabaceae*

GENUS *Acacia*

SPECIES *greggii*

OTHER NAMES wait-a-min-ute tree, paradise flower, devil acacia

to them, nutritious seed. They'd eat a bunch of pods and then wander off, depositing some of the undigested seeds in other places. Having been almost but not quite consumed in stomach acid, the seeds were then able to germinate and grow wherever they fell. Today, the seeds are washed and bumped and bruised as they head downstream but pretty much stay in the arroyos and ditches immersed in their favored alkali, gravelly soil; they grow but no longer expand their range. Not surprisingly, catclaw is one of the few legumes that does not fix nitrogen in the soil it grows in.

Catclaws' drought adaptation is most noticeable in the fact that they readily shed their leaves and keep them shed for much of the year. *Drought deciduous* it's called. Greening up and blooming is as much dependent on the rains of the previous fall as on those of the current spring. And some years the plants may actually throw their fragrant, pale yellow, sweet-smelling spikes of flowers twice, once due to the previous fall's moisture and again due to the current spring's moisture.

The size, fragrance, and abundance of the blooms have earned them another name: paradise flower. Their bloom times will vary, from April to October, but usually and mostly occur in April and May; a second bloom may come along in July and last for a bit. Once they begin blooming, they produce the most nectar when it is extremely dry, especially if there was a lot of rain the previous fall. Catclaws range from Texas to Southern California, north to Nevada and southern Colorado, and into Utah.

It's the thorns on these devils that earn them their name. Curved, like a cat's claw, and about the same size, they point upward, and they are sharp. When you pass by, they will snag clothes or, painfully, skin.

CATCLAW HONEY TASTING NOTES

WARM
ANIMAL
VEGETAL

Whether it's from Arizona or Texas, catclaw honey is viscous and sweet. If it was harvested in Texas, where it's called Uvalde honey, after the county, the color will be an ochre yellow that may remind you of sunshine. Catclaw from the desert Southwest will be much warmer and darker in color; think mahogany red. Both are richly flavored, with spicy and warm notes throughout. You'll think of cinnamon, maple syrup, and cooked butter, but the Southwest version drops in a little surprise at the finish, with notes of green vegetal and cough syrup that linger on the tongue. Texas catclaw honey has a brighter flavor than its desert sisters.

The full, rounded flavors and heavy texture of all catclaw honeys make them a tasty choice for drizzling over warm pecan pie or crème brûlée. For a real Texas tasting experience, add it to barbecue sauce for roasted ribs, and enjoy it with cornbread and baked beans.

GUAJILLO

FAMILY *Fabaceae*

GENUS *Acacia*

SPECIES *berlandieri*

OTHER NAMES thornless catclaw, mimosa catclaw, huajillo

This species occupies the smallest area of the four desert plants discussed here, ranging from the southwest portion of Texas west and south into Mexico for a bit, but only the northern third and eastern half of Mexico. It is nearly—but not quite—thornless; its thorns are short and curved, like those of the catclaw but shorter. This is a significant difference from its cousins, which are heavily armed. Guajillo grows up to fifteen feet tall, depending on available water, and thrives in well-drained, dry limestone hillsides with exceptionally shallow soil. It spreads profusely from its roots when in a favorable location. Because of its long bloom period, it is often used as an ornamental in the region; with proper pruning, it can be shaped and formed.

The round, whitish yellow, very sweetly scented flowers appear anytime between November and April, but February to April is most common. The honey is pure white, and, before the mesquite invasion, was a prime honey in that part of the world, with beekeepers able to make a year's income off a two-month bloom. Uvalde County, Texas, was famous for this particular honey, for both its color and its sublime flavor and aromas; trainloads were sold each season to honey packers in the North. This popularity was in part fueled by the stories of huge limestone caves filled with pure white honeycomb, guarded by ghosts and angry bees.

GUAJILLO HONEY TASTING NOTES

WARM FRUIT FLORAL

Guajillo is listed on Slow Food's Ark of Taste as one of the world's endangered honeys. It has a striking golden amber color with dusty orange tints. The nose will immediately draw you in with its warm spicy notes of cinnamon, peach, and dried fruit. Guajillo is a cloudy honey, and the texture is grippy on the tongue. Every spoonful is full of the same deep, complex flavors of spicy cinnamon and appealing notes of mango, apricot, and jammy cooked fruits so tangy they will make you want more. The flavors stay with you, and the finish leaves you with a metallic note and dry tongue similar to what you experience with unripened fruit. The honey is packed with pollen, evident in the first spoonful, which lingers in the back of your throat.

Guajillo honey is a fine accompaniment for ricotta cheese or Brie, pecans, crusty bread, and a glass of sangria or Beaujolais. Regional dishes with guajillo honey include heirloom, stone-ground, blue cornmeal pancakes with guajillo honey butter; and glazed pork with guajillo honey.

WHITE KIAWE

This mesquite relative was introduced to Hawaii in the 1820s by a Catholic missionary who brought it from Paris. It is native to northwest South America, where, interestingly, it is an endangered species. In Hawaii it is now considered naturalized, but it is an extremely invasive species of mesquite, a genus that has earned that distinction in many places in the world.

After introduction it soon became widespread. Used as a shade tree initially and as a good control for erosion, it eventually spread to the drier sides of all of the main islands of Hawaii. It grows anywhere from sea level to about two thousand feet and thrives where the rainfall is between ten and thirty inches a year. It does well in a mix of soils, from sandy and rocky, where it does all right, to deeper, slightly alkaline soils where it will grow to ninety feet and live more than a hundred years. It is one of very few plants that will do well in salt soil and even surrounded by salty water.

The wood is good for firewood and charcoal, and even furniture if it grows in protected locations, but on windy exposed slopes, it grows only a few feet high and is

FAMILY *Fabaceae*
GENUS *Prosopis*
SPECIES *pallida*
OTHER NAMES huarango, kawe

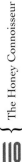

a twisted, dense shrub. Where it does well it forms very dense stands, spreading aggressively by both seed dispersal and from existing roots. It simply out-competes its neighbors for water, light, and nutrients and eventually stands alone. This competitiveness is an admirable trait when a high population is wanted but a noxious one when a clearing is overtaken.

Kiawe can thank the cattle industry for its success in Hawaii. When the industry discovered that cattle simply loved the highly nutritious seed pods, this invasive weedy tree rose to prominence; several hundred thousand acres were planted for cattle in the early 1930s. To make more pods from all these trees, growers needed honey bees for pollination. Hawaii's beekeepers rose to the occasion, their number growing exponentially in a few short years. Very soon Hawaii was exporting nearly a quarter million pounds a year of what turns out to be an excellent honey. But almost as fast, imported pests and diseases wreaked havoc on both the plants and the bees, and a once booming industry disappeared overnight. Only a few honey makers remain, still taking advantage of this wonderful honey.

Almost all honey varieties will granulate eventually. For some it takes years. For others, granulation can occur almost before the bees have capped the honey in the comb. Kiawe is such a honey. Today, a limited few beekeepers are able to time the harvest so that the honey is at exactly the right moisture content, before it crystalizes in the comb—a rare talent. However, the beauty of this honey, besides the flavor, is the tiny crystals found inside the honey that render it ultra-smooth and silky. Like a mouth full of butter, but, oh, so much better.

Threatened by urban expansion, the great stands of this once dominant plant will soon be gone, succumbing to golf courses and city streets. Kiawe honey's days are numbered, so hurry to try some.

KIAWE HONEY TASTING NOTES

WARM FRUIT FRESH

Honey from the kiawe plant is known as white kiawe honey. Something like a cross between white butter cream frosting and mascarpone cheese, white kiawe honey is nothing less than an utterly divine textural experience. Its white color is completely opaque, with a stunning pearlescent gloss. When you dip your spoon into the jar, be prepared to use a little wrist action to dig this honey out. Kiawe honey is more than thick; it's stiff enough to make firm peaks that will stand up and salute you. The texture is as smooth as a silk shirt, so don't waste any time getting this honey into your mouth. It arrives as a soft clump of cool sugar sweetness that almost chills your tongue until it dissolves, then magically evaporates. Delicately flavored and overly sweet, if you really concentrate you might notice the subtle flavor notes reminiscent of vanilla bean and wedding cake fondant. Otherwise, white kiawe honey is practically odorless and flavorless. The tasting experience is all about its dreamy texture. So if you are looking for something smoother and sweeter than granulated white sugar, get yourself some white kiawe honey.

Take advantage of kiawe's texture by spreading it on warm breads, cakes, and muffins. Use it as a substitute for frosting over your favorite baked goods. It's too good to just melt into a cup of tea; you can eat it straight like candy. It makes a good substitute for marshmallows in s'mores. Mix it with fresh garden herbs or add it to sliced fresh fruit.

MESQUITE

FAMILY *Fabaceae*
GENUS *Prosopis*
SPECIES *glandulosa*
OTHER NAMES honey mesquite

Not native to the United States, Mesquite moved north from Mexico into Louisiana and eastern Texas; west through New Mexico and Arizona and the Sonoran and Chihuahan deserts; into Southern California and north into Nevada, Utah, Colorado, and Oklahoma; and finally into southern Kansas and western Missouri.

Though there are several species, it's the honey mesquite that is the major nectar producer, and the major invasive species. Though competitive, it can't compete with native trees; so it has taken over what used to be miles of foraging grasslands for cattle. It also thrives in rocky, rough terrain, in washes and river bottoms with gravelly, stony soil. Essentially, it grows where native trees can't, and where it can outcompete less aggressive plants. This is true wherever it has been introduced; it is considered one of the world's most aggressive introduced species.

Honey mesquite will grow to thirty, even forty feet tall if there's enough moisture, and the root system of this plant is fascinating. The plant produces two kinds of roots, a set of deep roots that can penetrate even the hardest soil to depths of nearly two hundred feet to reach water, and a set of shallow roots that can soak up surface water in the rainy season. The plant can soak up surface water to the detriment of surrounding plants, to the point of dominating a landscape. The wood is sought after for firewood and to make barbecue briquettes for a "Southwest" smoked flavor, and the lumber can be used for implements and furniture.

On light, sandy soil, with ample moisture and rains, honey mesquite will grow to its fullest and will offer prodigious amounts of nectar when its typical yellowish spike flowers appear in the spring, at about the same time guajillo blooms where their locations overlap. In the area south and west of San Antonio, Texas, where this shrub thrives, honey mesquite produces an abundant honey crop nearly every year. But as it spreads, its popularity, along with its aggressiveness, continues to draw attention.

The seeds are high in sugar and favored by cattle, but they are also low in nutrition and can be toxic to cattle if eaten in a large quantity. The seeds can be ground for flour, as well, producing a sweet, somewhat nutty-flavored bread. Honey mesquite can be used as an ornamental, but use caution because the inch-long thorns are stout and dangerous—able to puncture tires, certainly shoes, and easily injure unprotected skin. The plant will form dense stands, like all of its cousins, by producing more plants from root buds and ample seeds.

MESQUITE HONEY TASTING NOTES

WARM
FRUIT
SPOILED

Mesquite honey is a remarkable homage to its desert terroir. It has a warm, dark mahogany color and a tantalizingly thick texture. It's so thick that you will not want to wait for it to pour, so have a spoon ready. The aroma reveals slight notes of yeast and baked white bread, but do not let that put you off. Mesquite is smooth and tastes of brown sugar or maple syrup. There are warm, musty grape notes throughout, but the syrup is what stays with you at the finish.

Mesquite honey pairs nicely with a Dutch goat Gouda cheese, whole grain breads, and malty brown ale. Mix mesquite with lime for a tangy glaze for smoked ham or a barbeque sauce for ribs. Drizzle on blue corn pancakes or corn muffins.

Chestnut honey is a staple in every Mediterranean kitchen. It is the last honey of the season to be extracted from the hives before they're prepared for winter. Its harvest is a sure sign that autumn has arrived, and it is widely celebrated with festivals throughout the region.

Castanea sativa originated in Europe, and its genus name, *Castanea*, comes from the town of Kastania in Thessaly, Greece. The chestnut is a deciduous tree that belongs to the Fagaceae family, a species of trees that includes oak and beech, and that bears edible nuts. The chestnut tree is valued for its hard wood, which is used to make barrels for aging balsamic vinegar, and for its large, edible nuts, a common culinary ingredient. The bark has deep furrows that form a crisscross pattern.

An ancient tree, the chestnut can live for five hundred years and usually does not begin to produce fruit until it is twenty years old, at which point it will remain productive for the rest of its existence. Chestnuts are forest trees that can grow over one hundred feet in height. They prefer the mild Mediterranean climate and enough moisture to support growth and nut production. They don't do well in lime soil and are sensitive to late spring and early winter frosts.

Chestnut flowers bloom from June till July, but the actual nut develops later that season, well after the honey harvest, inside a round, pale green, prickly shell. The tree bears flowers of long golden catkins that resemble mini bursts of fireworks; the leaves are oblong with serrated edges. Inside each shell are two or three oval-shaped nuts with white tips. Commercially grown, cultivated varieties, grown in Italy, Spain, France, and Portugal, produce only one large nut per shell.

FAMILY *Fagaceae*

GENUS *Castanea*

SPECIES *sativa* (European), *dentata* (American)

OTHER NAMES chinquapin chestnut, castagno, chat aignier, castano

CHESTNUT

The Honey Connoisseur

In the early 1900s a fungus brought to the United States on some chestnut trees imported from Asia nearly wiped out four billion of our native North America species (*Castanea dentata*). Efforts are being made to reintroduce a new hybrid of the American chestnut

When it's pure, chestnut honey exhibits the true chestnut flavor. It is one of the most sought-out honeys in the Mediterranean region because of its desirable dark color, which indicates a high level of antioxidants.

CHESTNUT HONEY TASTING NOTES

WOODY
WARM
ANIMAL

Not for the timid palate, chestnut honey's deep mahogany color hints at the heady flavors to come. This honey is sometimes opaque, and others times it is a transparent shade of brunette with red highlights. It is slow to crystallize, with a higher than usual water content of 20 percent. As you dip your spoon into the jar, you'll immediately notice its low viscosity, as the honey dribbles from your spoon before it reaches your mouth. Chestnut is either a honey you'll adore or one you'll wish you never met. The aromas are aggressively woody, pungent, and highly aromatic. The flavor releases quickly upon tasting and just might knock you over if you're not ready for a bittersweet tannic experience. Chestnut honey resonates with notes of carob, wet tobacco, and balsam and has overtones of smoke and leather. It is the bitter that lasts on your tongue.

Chestnut honey pairs well with savory foods rather than sweet and is a perfect partner for the deep flavors of autumn, drizzled over a wedge of Pecorino Toscano with some fresh pears or Gorgonzola on walnut bread, peppery arugula and cabernet sauvignon. Use it to lightly sweeten some black tea.

LING HEATHER

FAMILY *Ericaceae*

GENUS *Calluna*

SPECIES *vulgaris*

OTHER NAMES ling heather, Scottish Heather

There are three types of heathers found throughout Europe and the Irish and Scottish countrysides—ling heather (*Calluna vulgaris*), bell heather (*Erica cinerea*), and cross-leaved heather (*Erica tetralix*). Ling heather is the only species in the genus *Calluna* and is generally known as heather. *Callunas* are differentiated from *Ericas*, or heaths, by their upright branches and tiny overlapping leaves that resemble scales; the leaves of Erica are fine textured and needle like.

Ling is a hardy perennial that flourishes in dry, sandy soils that are acidic and depleted of minerals. It tolerates extreme temperatures and the strong winds typical of the moors where it grows. Ling will live up to fifty years if left alone, but stands are burned every ten to twelve years to prevent older shrubs from taking over the moor and to encourage new growth, essential to the wildlife that uses heather for food and cover.

Heather is heavily grazed by cattle, and burning also reduces tall plants that predators use for cover.

Mature plants have woody stems that intertwine tightly and grow up to thirty-six inches tall. All heathers have tiny flowers, and all are important sources of pollen and nectar for honey bees. When heather blooms, the moors and heathland scrub are a carpet of pink, mauve, and occasionally white flowers. Ling is the last of the heathers to bloom, beginning in late July, peaking in August, and finishing in September. Although ling has a relatively long blooming period, nectar secretion is confined to only four or five days. In order to harvest ling honey, local beekeepers like to say that they must go early in the morning early in August and leave late in the evening late in September.

LING HONEY TASTING NOTES:

WOODY ANIMAL WARM

Ling honey is highly regarded; some connoisseurs call it the Rolls-Royce of honeys because of its rich flavors and unique characteristics. It has an extremely viscous, jellylike texture. Open a jar and turn it upside down; Ling honey refuses to pour out. It actually sticks to the inside of the jar. This property of thixotrophy, as mentioned previously, allows the honey to become liquid when it is stirred or vibrated but return to jelly when standing still. One way to test ling's purity is by scraping a line on the surface of the honey to see how quickly it fills in. If the line stays on the surface, it's not mixed with other heather honeys. Another quality of pure ling honey is the presence of tiny air bubbles throughout. Beekeepers often hand-press ling honey from the combs to separate it from the wax, creating bubbles inside the honey. Thixotrophy is why you will often find ling sold inside the original comb.

Ling is dark amber and absolutely opaque. The aroma is intense, full of earthy and woody notes with hints of burnt caramel or sugar. Not surprisingly, it's chewy, and with a water content of approximately 23 percent, it neither ferments nor crystallizes. A spoonful delivers pungent flavors of warm and smoky toffee that you will adore or abhor. Underneath you'll discover fruity plum, blackberry, and bitter coffee flavors that will grow on you. The finish is slightly chemical with a tanginess that lingers. This is a sophisticated honey for those who enjoy deep, bitter flavors.

Ling honey should be paired with Stilton or cheddar cheese. Drizzle heather honey over porridge, Scottish griddle cakes, or seared salmon.

Bell heather is a close relative of ling found in the British Isles, but the honey has very different sensory qualities. It is reddish in color and transparent, resembling port wine. It's also thinner than ling and is extracted with traditional equipment. The aroma is strong, woody, and refreshing. The flavor is bitter, with perfumy and floral notes. It has hints of mint not found in ling. Samuel Adams Honey Porter beer is brewed with Scottish heather honey, as is Drambuie.

Besides the Eiffel Tower, is there anything more French than lavender? The world-renowned lavender fields of Provence have been an inspirational destination for painters and tourists from every corner of the earth. Lavender is a cultural icon in Provence, and all things lavender command premium prices, including the honey.

There are close to thirty species of lavender, with purple, pink, or white flowers. The queen of the French lavender industry is pure *lavandula augustiflora*; even though it is not the most prolific, it is the only one granted the appellation *d'origine contrôlée* (AOC), or controlled designation of origin, by the French government, which occurred in 1981. Lavender honey also has a respected status indigenous to France; the *Label rouge* certification guarantees the origin, purity, and quality of taste of Provence's terroir honey.

Lavender is a small, herbaceous, shrubby plant that is highly aromatic. It has slender leaves and thin, dense, spiky stalks with flowers that grow in tiny fragrant clumps. It grows wild from June to August near the seacoast in the south of France, where the summers are extremely arid. The south of France is a geographically protected eco-region surrounded by mountains, where sunny exposures meet the gentle Mediterranean winds. The dry, rocky limestone the French call *garrigue*, which is similar to California's chaparral soil, makes a perfect home for the heat-loving lavender plant.

When lavender is at peak bloom, the sight of its purple carpets is breathtaking, and the aroma is intoxicating; it is the signature scent of Provence. Lavender flowers are irresistible to honey bees. Beekeepers monitor their beehives closely during lavender production by weighing them every two days to measure the nectar flow and determine how

LAVENDER

GENUS *Lavandula*
SPECIES *angustifolia*
OTHER NAMES *lavanda, lavande, espliego*

quickly bees are bringing in nectar. After the bloom the lavender honey is removed from the hives and regularly checked by third parties that monitor the origin and quality of the honey, especially in regard to taste.

FRESH FLORAL WOODY

If you've never been to Provence, a jar of lavender honey is the next best thing. It purely expresses the terroir of the south of France. The finest lavender honey is transparent, white with tinges of golden sunshine. Honey harvested closer to the sea is often darker. When it crystallizes, it is fine, with a smooth mouth feel. The Mediterranean sun fills each bottle with the scent of lavender fields. Open the jar, close your eyes, and breathe deeply to catch the heady aromas of soft florals, camphor, almond, and vanilla. The flavor is delicate and slightly acidic, with floral and perfumed notes.

Lavender honey pairs with roasted figs, gingerbread, blue-veined and goat cheeses, chamomile tea, and vanilla ice cream. It also mixes well in salad dressings. Classic French recipes made with lavender honey include nougats, crepes, and their famous pain *d'épices*, or gingerbread.

LEATHERWOOD

FAMILY *Cunoniaceae*
GENUS *Eucryphia*
SPECIES *lucida*
OTHER NAMES swamp gum, mountain ash

Just like clockwork, every January, on the Australian island state of Tasmania some 17,000 beehives are trucked to the northwest region to begin the most important beekeeping activity on the island: harvesting Tasmania's legendary leatherwood honey. Tasmanian beekeepers build up their colonies all year in preparation for the highly anticipated leatherwood bloom. The state's two hundred beekeepers will migrate their colonies west into the pristine rain forest of such places as Tarkine and South West Wilderness, then camp out until early March, when the nectar flow expires. Leatherwood honey has an illustrious reputation around the world, and as a $4 million industry, it makes up more than two thirds of all the honey produced on the island.

Leatherwood is a stately evergreen endemic to Tasmania and has been around for 65 million years. It is no wonder that the state government controls the commercial beekeeping industry, and the very rain forests where leatherwood grows are

now designated World Heritage sites. The leatherwood bloom season is short, and the densely vegetated region where the trees flourish is isolated and extremely rugged. These areas are far from human intervention and extremely difficult to access, even for beekeepers.

There are two types of leatherwood trees, *Eucryphia lucida* and *Eucryphia milliganii,* but it is *E. lucida* that is vital to leatherwood honey production. This species usually grows only six to thirty feet but can reach heights of eighty feet. Both species are shade tolerant and grow in the understory of the rain forest canopy, below the majestic Tasmanian oak trees. The leatherwood tree prefers a cool, rainy, and wet climate and an acidic soil, which the rain forest provides beautifully. The tree is named for the tough texture of its leaves, fruit, and flower petals. The bark of the tree is wrinkled and dark green, sometimes brown or gray, and is often covered with lichens. Leatherwood trees have long, thick, oval-shaped leaves, a brilliant shade of green with gray underneath. It bears strikingly large, pale pink, rose-like flowers, which make the tree appear almost completely white from a distance. The nectary emits a distinctive spicy aroma that permeates the humid forest air; inside it are hundreds of red-tipped stamens that form a global shape. When in full bloom, leatherwood produces generous amounts of nectar that practically drips from the flowers, just waiting for the honey bees. *E. lucida* is an ancient tree that grows slowly and reaches maturity at 250 years. Nectar secretion is substantial in only those trees over 75 years old, so the honey industry relies on the mature trees. The bloom is unpredictable, but beekeepers believe a wet autumn and spring bring a bountiful nectar flow. They swear that at night the sound of the bees flapping their wings to evaporate the moisture and ripen the nectar is like a lion's roar.

Producing this fine leatherwood honey was not always a smooth undertaking,

Leatherwood timber from the oldest trees is highly sought after by loggers, who use it for pulpwood and manufacturing fine furniture. This activity put Tasmania's most famous honey industry at risk and was a threat to the rain forest where leatherwood grows, until it was designated as a botanically unique World Heritage Zone in 1982. Efforts by the locals continue in an attempt to stop the destruction of the unspoiled land that the logging industry is still slowly depleting. Although Tasmania boasts other nectar sources for apiculture, such as field clover, blackberry, and twenty-seven species of eucalyptus, leatherwood is a cultural icon.

LEATHERWOOD HONEY TASTING NOTES

WOODY FRESH ANIMAL

Leatherwood honey crystallizes, or as the natives say, " candies," very quickly, so it is in that state that you most likely will encounter it. In its liquid form, it's an ochre-yellow to deep reddish amber color that is fairly transparent and viscous. Opening up a jar of leatherwood honey is like taking a trip to the wild woodlands of the rain forest but with an edge. You cannot ignore the heady aromatic balsamic notes that smell of an evergreen tree and grape juice. The flavor of leatherwood is intense, clearly musky and woody, with warm hints of anise and camphor that persist on the tongue. Did we forget to mention that leatherwood honey tastes, well, a bit like leather? The whole experience is complex and leaves spicy and peppery notes that linger in the throat.

Pair leatherwood honey with a native Tasmanian or any smoked cheddar and a native pinot noir. Traditional Tasmanian recipes call for date pudding with leatherwood honey. It is also used to brew ginger beers and ales.

FAMILY *Myrtaceae* (myrtle family)

GENUS *Leptospermum*

SPECIES *scoparium*

OTHER NAMES tea tree, New Zealand honeysuckle, broom tea tree, kahikatoa, red tea tree, red manuka

MANUKA

Mysterious and magical, manuka honey has a worldwide reputation as the honey that heals. It is well known that honey has been used for thousands of years as a medical treatment. Today, doctors around the world write prescriptions for manuka honey for patients suffering from a wide range of illnesses; it has been proven to have supernatural healing properties. It is produced from the commonly named tea tree, which is known for its antimicrobial, antifungal, and antibacterial benefits. It was dubbed "tea tree" by the eighteenth-century explorer Captain Cook, who made a tea by infusing the leaves in hot water. Beekeepers set their hives close to tea trees for only six weeks for the bees to gather the nectar. Nine to twelve thousand tons of manuka honey is produced annually, with almost one-third to one-half exported, much of it for the pharmaceutical industry. *Manuka* is the name given to *L. scoparium* by the Maori, indigenous Polynesian people of New Zealand. It is native to New Zealand and Australia. This prolific evergreen shrub grows from six to sixteen feet. Lowland alpine regions and the shrubland alpine forests are ideal for the manuka tree. Commonly found in wetland areas and on dry hillsides, it also can thrive on sandy coastal woodlands in temperate maritime climates typical of the Stewart Islands and Tasmania. Once mature, it is tolerant of many growing conditions. It can withstand high-acid and low-fertility soils, and even areas exposed to frost and wind or the salt sprays from the South Pacific Ocean. Manuka was once treated as a weed because it grows uncultivated throughout the country; it is now considered an important part of the ecosystem, however, because it is a pioneer-ing species that grows rapidly to regenerate low-nutrient land that has eroded or been cleared by fire for pasture. Manuka also tends to overshadow other native species, acting as a protective canopy, but once the surrounding plants mature, it dies from lack of essential sunshine and therefore has a short life cycle.

Manuka's flowers are quite large and showy, with five white to blush-pink petals filled with red stamens and white pollen, important for the many native pollinators. During the Australian summer, September through June, manuka blooms profusely, giving off a magnificent ginger-peppery aroma. The narrow, sharp-tipped leaves are aromatic, too; they feature oil glands that emit a camphorous scent reminiscent of myrtle. In autumn, the seeds ripen inside a brown acorn-like capsule but are not released until the following year. The bark is usually covered with a black, sooty fungus that survives on the honeydew produced by the scale insects that inhabit the tree. Ma-nuka has a lovely brownish pinkish wood that is tough and hard with an interesting grain; it is used for fencing and tool handles and for smoking fish and meat.

In order for a honey to be labeled as manuka, at least 70 percent of its pollen con-tent must come from *Leptospermum scoparium*. Manuka is also rated with a number known as the Unique Manuka Factor (UMF), which measures the potency of its antibacte-rial properties. The UMF name is a regis-tered trademark, and only those producers that qualify can license it to market their honey. The UMF number begins at 10+ and can be as high as 40+. The higher the number, the higher the concentrate, and the more costly the manuka honey.

MANUKA HONEY TASTING NOTES

ANIMAL WOODY CHEMICAL WARM

Manuka honey is typically packed in dark jars to protect it from light, which will compromise its active enzymes and antibacterial activity. So you will have to open a jar to see its deep hazelnut color and experience its aggressive and heady aromas.

Manuka smells like damp earth, burnt sugar, and camphor herbs, and its flavors are just as bold. It is a thixotropic honey that has a thick and delightfully creamy texture that will granulate rather quickly. If it's crystallized, the granules might be some-what harsh on your tongue. The flavor is of musty wood and caramelized sugars, with notes of pepper and ginger. As it melts in your mouth, you will discover the flavor of sweet flowers, but that disappears with the honey, leaving a somewhat bitter taste on your tongue. This is a bold honey, for those who prefer honey with a deep, savory edge.

Manuka honey is used by locals in many culinary dishes and beverages. Its deep earthy flavors complement minted lamb, beef, and ginger salmon dishes. Another favorite is a Stilton and pear tart in pine nut pastry with manuka honey. Traditional mixed drinks that call for manuka honey are a lemon and ginger hot toddy and a maple sour cocktail made with vodka, lemon juice, and a dash of bitters.

FAMILY *Rhamnaceae*

GENUS *Ziziphus*

SPECIES *spina-christi*

OTHER NAMES lote, jujube, nabbag, nabkh, al-sidr tree

SIDR

Deeply rooted in the Arabic culture for centuries and more precious than oil, sacred sidr honey from Hadramaut in the southwestern Arabian Peninsula, is the most sought-after honey in the entire world, commanding astronomical prices. As we write this, one kilo (2.2 pounds) of sidr honey is selling for US$250. It has become a status symbol among the wealthy elite. Beekeepers remain vigilant and even armed throughout the season to protect their beehives, with the belief that sidr honey is a gift directly from Allah.

The sidr tree, also called jujube or Christ's thorn, is named after the very thorny branches that were woven into the crown placed on Jesus Christ's head before his crucifixion. This venerable evergreen is native to the Sudan yet grows extensively in the eastern part of Yemen and the moun-

tains of Hadramaut in the uncultivated desert. The sidr tree prefers full sun, parched air, and the sandy soil typical of the deserts of Yemen, making it an extremely drought-tolerant honey plant. Beekeepers claim that the sidr honey harvested from the Yemen region tastes superior to the sidr harvested from any other region, specifically because of the terroir. Sidr is a deep-rooted tree with a wide, brown, wrinkled trunk that grows between twenty-one and twenty-four feet high. The relatively large oval-shaped green leaves have deep veins and hang from gray, spindly branches, making the tree appear scrubby. The flowers are much smaller than the leaves and appear as pale yellowish green clusters growing very close to the branches. Each flower produces a round, green edible fruit that resembles an apple, which turns yellow-orange when mature.

Twice every year, in the winter and again in summer, beekeepers living around Yemen haul their wooden or terra cotta hives on top of their cars or pickup trucks through the countryside and up the rugged Hadramaut mountains to secure their treasure. Producing sidr honey is labor intensive; the harvest is extremely limited yet worth the effort to acquire the most esteemed honey in the world. The bloom will last up to sixty days, but the most nectar is secreted by the elder plants ten days into the bloom. Although some beekeepers reap up to five honey harvests each season in Yemen, it is the winter shatwi (winter) honey that is revered as the finest.

Yemeni beekeepers are strict to ensure their honey's purity and would rather allow their bees to starve than feed them with sugar syrup when flower nectar is not available. They do not allow the use of antibiotics inside their hives, and the mountainous region where the sidr trees grow is pesticide free. Honey is extracted from the comb by gently squeezing it by hand to obtain the liquid. Harvesting honey has been done this way in Yemen for seven thousand years. The most important bee species in Yemen is *Apis mellifera yemenitica*, which has a small dark abdomen with gray stripes.

The tradition of keeping bees is passed down through generations. Beekeepers are highly respected and make a good living selling their liquid gold. Honeycomb is packed in metal tins and liquid honey in glass bottles. Both are sold at local outdoor markets called souks or at auction in other countries, mainly to Saudi princes. Honey stores are common in the Yemeni region, and customers make trips specifically to purchase this desirable honey for their households. Sidr honey is a sign of prestige and a common wedding gift. Shopkeepers offer tastings of each vintage of honey, acknowledging the differences in color, aroma, and flavor. Quality is important to the consumer, and honey in the comb is the preferred type, as it is the closest to what the bees produced. Customers are quite knowledgeable; it is common for customers to test the honey before making a purchase by dripping a small amount onto the dry, dusty ground. If it remains in a ball rather than spreading out, it is believed to be pure.

SIDR HONEY TASTING NOTES:

FRUIT
WARM
WOODY

What would you expect the most extravagant honey in the world to taste like? Sidr honey from Yemen is deep, rich amber in color, reminiscent of dark chocolate syrup. Sidr from other regions can be a lighter amber with reddish tints. It whispers the warm earthy and sandy aromas of the Hadramaut Desert in every drop. It is thick enough to stick to your spoon without a drip. It is deeply flavored, with a long flavor release, as its very thick texture takes a few seconds to melt on the tongue. Once this honey reaches body temperature, you register the sweet hints of apple laced with dried dates and the buttery treacle or golden syrup popular in the United Kingdom. It is nicely balanced, and you are left with a syrupy flavor that lingers. Sidr honey is believed to have many medicinal benefits and an unusually high level of antioxidants. It is marketed as a cure for many illnesses and is also believed by the locals to have aphrodisiac qualities.

Sidr is traditionally eaten by dipping warm bread into the honey and sprinkling nigella seeds on top. Two popular recipes include *bint al sahan*, a pastry drizzled with honey, and *fatteh bi'asil*, milk and bread with honey.

FAMILY *Lamiaceae*

GENUS *Thymus*

SPECIES *vulgaris*

OTHER NAMES Breckland thyme, wild thyme, creeping thyme

THYME

Thyme honey has been praised for its heady aroma since ancient times and is a staple in Greek kitchens. It is also known as Hymettus honey after the mountain range in Attica, Greece, just southeast of Athens. Thyme is part of the mint family and is cultivated for its pungent-smelling essential oil, which is used as both a culinary and a medicinal herb. There are hundreds of varieties of thyme, and their nectar is highly attractive to honey bees. Wild thyme (*Thymus serpyllum*) and common thyme (*Thymus vulgaris*) are the most widely cultivated species, blooming from June to July. These perennials are native to Europe and North Africa. *Serpyllum* is derived from the Greek work meaning "to creep."

Thyme is a low-growing evergreen shrub that is often used as ground cover. It is very hardy and grows in almost any soil type but prefers the well-drained rocky earth around Greece's limestone mountains. Mounds of wild thyme can be found even clinging to crevices and along the sandy hills sloping down to the shoreline. These areas are barren most of the year until the thyme flowers bloom. The warm, arid climate of the Mediterranean is perfect for this plant, because thyme needs extended periods of full sun to thrive and be flavorful. Yet thyme can be surprisingly versatile and tolerate periods of drought and even deep freezes. It is easily identified by its woody stalks and tiny green-gray leaves that emit a pungent herbal, lemon-like aroma. Its small flowers bloom in dense heads, covering entire hillsides with carpets of purple, pale pink, or white.

THYME HONEY TASTING NOTES

FRESH
WOODY
FRUIT

There is a saying that goes "If olive oil is the lifeline of Greece, then honey is the soul." If you're looking for a richly flavored honey with lots of personality, thyme honey is worth a try. Very aromatic and intense, this Greek treasure, usually sold in small decorative metal cans, is a worldwide favorite. It has a deep, heady scent that is full of warm fruit and reminiscent of menthol and pine resin. Light to medium amber in color and full bodied, thyme honey turns varying shades of beige and red when it crystallizes. The crystals could be somewhat coarse on your tongue, but the flavor is still heavenly. The first spoonful delivers a sweet, camphorous flavor that is woody and fresh, surrounded by cooked fruit. As it fades, you are left with a refreshing note. Overall, there's a distinct hint of the herb that gives thyme honey a sophisticated appeal.

Thyme honey drizzled over thick, creamy Greek yogurt is a timeless pairing. Traditional Greek offerings are *melopita*, a honey cake; baklava; or roasted feta drizzled with thyme honey.

ULMO

FAMILY *Cunoniaceae*

GENUS *Eucryphia*

SPECIES *cordifolia*

OTHER NAMES gnulgu, muermo, roble de Chile

Beginning every January, the majestic ulmo tree spreads her fragrant white flowers like a morning mist across the hills of the Chilean rain forest. It is summer, and the ulmo flowers are in full bloom and covered with honey bees that produce the exquisite and rare ulmo honey adored all over the European Union. The ulmo is an evergreen tree of the Cunoniaceae family of woody plants and is endemic to the pristine rain forests around the lakes region of Chile. It is also found growing as far south as Isla de Chiloé and the historical region of Araucanía. Towering up to sixty-five feet high, the ulmo tree is supported by a thick brown trunk with wrinkled bark that resembles the skin of an elephant. This hardwood tree is a favorite of loggers, who seek out its attractive reddish brown lumber because of the desirable smooth grain that is resistant to moisture and decay. Indigenous to Argentina as well as Chile, the ulmo tree displays flashy white clusters of anemone flowers with hundreds of stamens. They are highly aromatic and produce copious amounts of nectar, making them attractive to honey bees. The fruit is a red capsule that produces winged seeds, which don't drop until the following year. Ulmo leaves are spade shaped, dense, and leathery, with serrated edges.

Chile is a thin strip of land, an isolated valley with rolling hills that lies between the Andes Mountain range and the South Pacific Ocean. This unique location gives it a wide variation in temperatures and a rich environment for bees to pollinate the diverse agricultural crops that the country is known for. *Ulmo* means "elm." The tree thrives in an acidic soil that is rich in organic material. Preferring a humid environment with constant rainfall balanced with full sun, it can tolerate occasional freezing spells but not a winter snowfall. The cool ocean breeze, locally known as the *selva fría*, or cold forest, blows from the west off the Pacific. This, along with Chile's proximity to the mountains, creates the perfect terroir for the ulmo tree.

Beekeeping has a long tradition in Chile. Legend has it that the Italian honey bee *Apis mellifera ligustica* was brought to the city of Peñaflor in the mid-1800s by an unknown sailor. Only two of those colonies survived, and they adapted very nicely to Chile's extremely biodiverse rain forest, including its native ulmo tree. Today, beekeepers that produce this rain forest honey manage their colonies using the traditional Langstroth hives, which are commonly painted in bright and cheerful colors. Ulmo honey production is a multimillion dollar industry, and the European Union is the largest consumer. Often Chilean honey contains genetically modified (GM) pollen and must be labeled as such so it can be sold in the European Union. GM crops are widely grown in Chile but not for human consumption. A computerized tracking system named the

National Geographic System for Apiculture Consultation has been put into place by the Chilean agriculture and livestock service to track where GM crops are being grown. This program helps beekeepers find suitable areas to stage their hives that are far enough away from GM crops and transgenic pollen, which would contaminate their honey. Chilean beekeepers are now trying to aquire certification to protect the geographic origin and quality of their untainted ulmo honey.

Largely unknown in the United States, ulmo honey was the named the Best Raw Honey of 2007 at the San Francisco Fancy Food Show, launching it as a must-try Chilean honey among food and cheese lovers around the country. Research has shown that ulmo honey has health benefits that rival that of New Zealand's manuka.

caramel. It all disappears rather quickly, but the brown sugar note lingers. There's a sharp but pleasant burn in your throat as the honey goes down.

Pair ulmo honey with traditional Chilean Chanco or Panquehue cheese, vanilla ice cream, *dulce de leche*, rice pudding, flan, or corn cakes, or use it to make savory sauces for fish. Local Chilean recipes include ulmo honey cookies and a traditional drink called an ulmo pisco sour, a yellow grape brandy drink made with lemon juice, egg whites, and ulmo honey.

ULMO HONEY TASTING NOTES

WARM
FLORAL
FRUIT
VEGETAL

The name *ulmo* might be difficult to remember, but its flavor is unforgettable. The color is a maize yellow, resembling lemon curd. It's a drippy and sticky honey, yet thick enough to hold a toothpick. Its initial aroma brings to mind rubber tires, but it does get better, and by the third whiff you'll recognize earthier fruity notes trailing behind. Once the honey is in your mouth, you'll want to massage its fine crystalized granules between your tongue and palate to savor its jammy texture. Ulmo honey immediately delivers strong and persistent flavors to your tongue. As it melts, you'll recognize warm aniseed and short floral notes of jasmine, with a touch of black tea and

Mad Honey

Throughout history there have been tales about toxic reactions by humans to certain types of honeys produced by bees that collect nectar from poisonous plants. This is often known as "mad honey poisoning." The plants are mainly of the Ericaceae family and include azalea, mountain laurel, rhododendron, oleander, sheep laurel, and tutu bush. Due to a compound called grayanotoxins found in the honey, which acts on the nervous system, an innocent sip could kill a horse or render a soldier senseless for more than twenty-four hours. The first known incident was recorded in Xenophon's book *Anabasis*. In 401 BC Xenophon was leading ten thousand mercenaries back to Greece after fighting the grand army of Persia when they made camp in the ancient territory of Colchis (in western Georgia). They stumbled upon some wild beehives and feasted on the honey. Within minutes the soldiers became intoxicated madmen and then collapsed. Fortunately, they recovered a few days later. Four centuries later, three Roman squadrons under General Pompey were not as lucky. While campaigning against King Mithridates at Trebizond on the south shore of the Black Sea, they encountered some toxic honeycombs left out by the Heptakometes, allies of Mithridates. When Pompey's men devoured the honey, they were rendered senseless and unable to defend themselves, at which time they were massacred by Mithridates' troops.

Today, incidents of grayanotoxins poisoning are rare, and you won't find mad honey in your local market. However, there are several types of rhododendron in the United States that produce grayanotoxins. Along the West Coast there is the western azalea (*Rhododendron occidentale*), California rosebay (*Rhododendron macrophyllum*), and Cascade azalea (*Rhododendron albiflorum*). In the eastern part of the country, look out for mountain laurel (*Kalmia latifolia*) and sheep laurel (*Kalmia angustifolia*).

Most cases of mad honey poisoning have been reported in Turkey. The cause is usually honey from Turkey's native *Rhododendron ponticum* growing on the east and south side of the Black Sea, a region notorious for poisonous plants.

Mountain laurel is not an attractive plant to honey bees and they will avoid it if anything else is blooming, which is usually the case. However, if a late frost kills the early plants, the frost tolerant mountain laurel is all that remains. Bees will visit the mountain laurel out of necessity. The resulting honey does not harm honey bees, but if pure enough, causes mouth numbness and discomfort swallowing in humans. No known cases of poisoning have occurred because fast growing colonies usually consume the honey instead of storing it. Occasionally though a beekeeper, curious as to what the bees have found, will encounter this honey and be surprised by the tingling on the tongue and the numbness of lips that it causes.

CHAPTER } 4

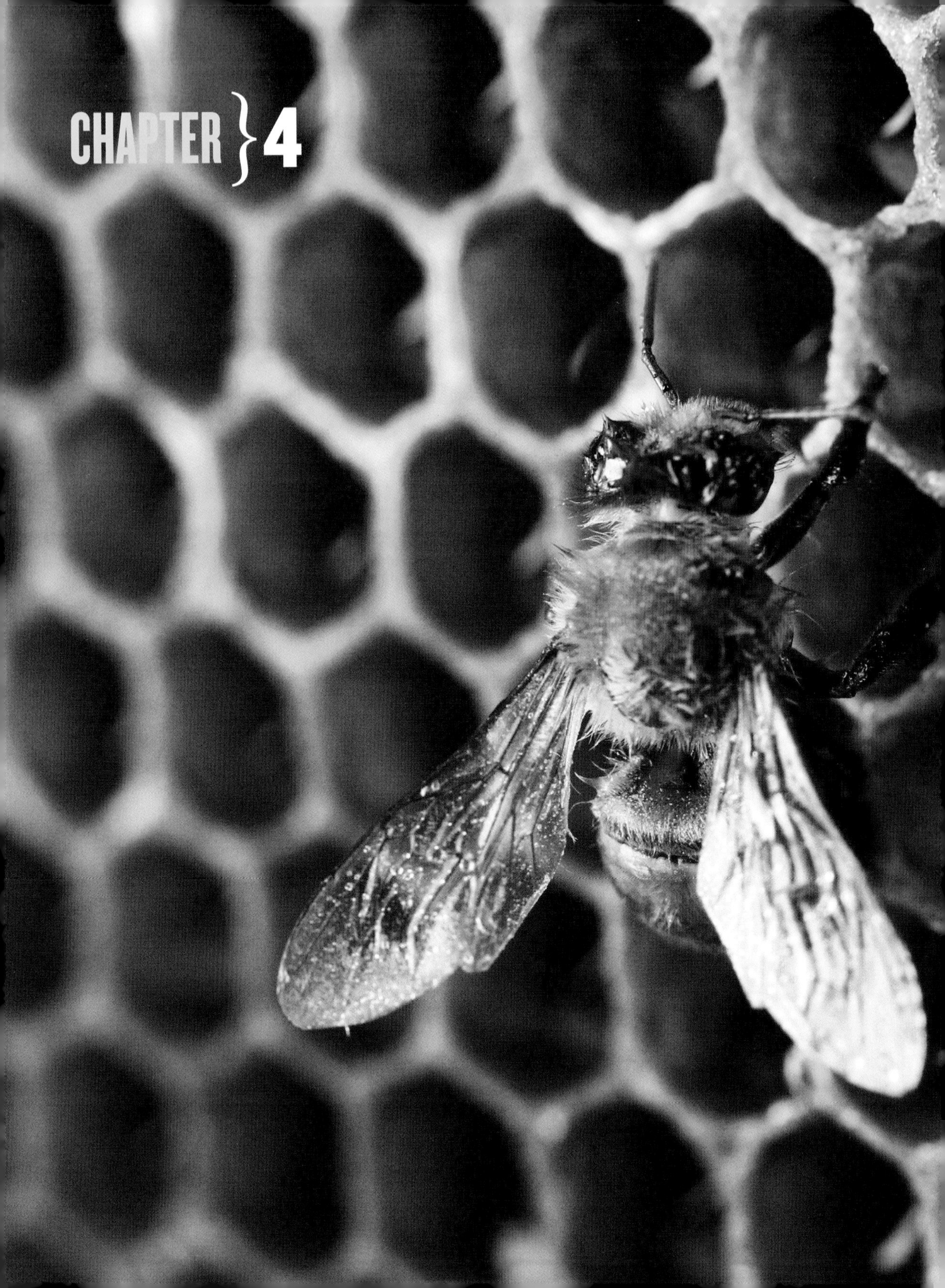

THE NOT-SO-SWEET
SIDE OF HONEY

Honey bees are the descendants of carnivorous, wasp-like creatures that, millions of years ago, found it more practical to become vegetarians and exploit a rapidly evolving plant world than to remain hunters competing in a limited-prey ecosystem. It's believed that they began their journey in east central Africa and, after becoming established, gradually migrated south, west, and eventually north in search of food and space.

Leaving Africa, they headed across the Mediterranean to what are now the Italian and Iberian peninsulas. From there they migrated to the mountainous regions of what has become southeastern Europe and northwest into southern, central, and western Europe. Each of these environments—tropical, sub-tropical, mountainous, and eventually the moderate climates of western and central Europe—left an evolutionary mark, and thus a unique race, or species, of honey bee evolved in each region.

Several species of honey bees remain in Asia and Africa. Some build nests of a single beeswax comb on high tree limbs, or even on the sides of cliffs. These are harvested by local people who climb the trees or cliffs protected only by the smoke of the burning branches they carry. They wear very little in the way of protective gear. Finding wild bee nests in dense jungles can be difficult, but a bird known as a honeyguide has learned to attract the attention of hunting groups and lead them to their goal. When the nests are harvested the bird enjoys the remains, which include the dead bees and any bits of wax, honey, and especially larvae that are not taken away. Everybody wins except the bees.

Though the nests are destroyed in the process and little is harvested from each nest, often many nests exist in a location, and a fair quantity of honey can be gathered during a single robbing inciden; along with the honey, the comb containing brood is taken, since larvae are a viable source of protein.

Most of the races of bees that remain in southern Africa and the tropical world have an army of natural predators, including man. It is defend or die, and those that are the strongest, the bravest, and the meanest survive.

The bees that eventually moved into southern and central Europe were forced to adapt to a very different geography and climate. Because these northern regions experience longer and more discrete seasons—typically winter, spring, summer, and autumn, with spring and summer, and sometimes autumn, offering foraging and flying weather—the bees developed the instinct to store food produced during the warm seasons to consume when winter's grip kept them from flying and plants from growing. This instinct, called hoarding, is what enables honey bees to survive harsh winters, not as a solitary queen hiding under the bark of a tree, as in the case of many solitary bees and wasps, but as a thriving community, raising young and functioning as a colony. This characteristic is what attracts us to the honey bee. We provide a safe, healthy place for the bees to live, protection from pests and predators, and management practices that ensure that they thrive. In return, we can, with care and consideration, harvest from the bees the surplus honey they have worked hard to produce, and still leave behind more than enough for them to dine on all winter long.

Today honey bees live on every continent in the world except the Arctic and Antarctic.

Today honey bees live on every continent in the world except the Arctic and Antarctic. Between these polar locations have evolved dozens of races (subspecies, actually) of honey bees that are able to nest, reproduce, and produce honey in their chosen climate, geography, and terrain.

Over the eons individual beekeepers have selected the best traits from many of these races in an effort to breed a creature that best suits the location in which the bee collects nectar and produces honey. The environment of northern Europe is much different than that of central Texas, for example, while Southern California is unlike Maine. Breeding the best bee for one's location has become a necessary skill for beekeepers to be successful. Experimenting with races from different environments, or hybrids of several races, has proven both profitable and productive, but the process continues to be a work in progress.

Even so, in most places in the world honey can be produced in abundance when proper equipment and management techniques are employed. Introducing honey bees to people not familiar with them, or unfamiliar with honey as a food, has been especially successful in cultures where women are not a common part of the work force but care for the children and gardens. After all, beekeeping does not require a large investment in equipment or any more land than a garden plot to be successful. Micro-loans and local co-ops are helping cottage industries grow in many places, and because there is generally a market for honey and beeswax, they provide a means for women to improve the lives of their families. But just as often men dominate the

beekeeping scene, and, since there is often little in the way of formal training, skills are passed from father to son, with little change in technique or skill. In almost all of the locations where that occurs, some beekeepers still keep their bees in traditional beehives made of clay, logs, or simple boxes the way their parents and grandparents did, slowing the advancement of both the community and beekeeping.

Despite some pockets of long-held traditions surrounding beekeeping practices, beekeepers worldwide have mostly adopted both modern management skills and equipment, including the movable frame hive. Most of the bees used are derived from the group that landed in central Europe and have been exported to every corner of the habitable world. They tend to be more gentle than not and honey hoarders rather than migrators, unlike their African forbears. These bees efficiently produce large crops of honey, some of which is consumed locally but much of which is gathered by honey exporters to send to countries that cannot or do not produce enough honey to meet the local demand.

The United States is one of those countries, and not surprisingly, as with much of our agricultural production, honey consumption and production in the U.S. has evolved in the past few decades. In the 1970s and 1980s U.S. beekeepers produced about 220 million pounds of honey a year, and an additional 50 million pounds were imported to meet local demand. But in 2011 U.S. beekeepers produced only 150 million pounds of honey, while nearly 290 million pounds were imported to meet the demand. True, there are more people living in the United States now—over 300 million—but we consumed about 440 million pounds of honey in 2011, about a pound and a quarter per person, up from just barely a pound per person thirty years ago. More people are eating more honey in this country, creating a huge opportunity for American honey pro-

ducers that has yet to be fully exploited.

So where does all that imported honey come from? To be able to produce, harvest, process, and transport large honey crops requires a cooperative climate, productive bees, and a significant investment in hardware, starting with thousands, perhaps millions of modern beehives, each producing to its best potential, as much as 200 to 250 pounds of honey a year. Once produced, the honey must be harvested, processed, and stored in barrels or tankers ready to sell. There must be adequate transportation infrastructure to get it from where it is produced to a port capable of shipping it internationally. All of this requires reliable power, an adequate communication infrastructure, and sufficient capital. Not every country in the world is capable of these operations, but nearly forty countries have enough of them in place to export honey to our shores. Some countries send as little as 500–600 pounds (a gallon of honey weighs in at 12 pounds, so a 55-gallon drum weighs 660 pounds), while others send millions and millions of pounds. Of the 289 million pounds we imported in 2011, 227 million pounds, or 79 percent, came from just four countries—Argentina, Brazil, India, and Vietnam. Canada and Mexico were a distant fifth and sixth, and, because of import restrictions, once powerful China played hardly a role at all, unless you consider its 20 million pounds that were illegally imported, found, and confiscated.

Illegitimate Honey

Almost all of the honey imported to the United States is legitimate and good quality, but illegitimate honey is a problem. A recent U.S. Department of Homeland Security report indicates that honey is one of the four most adulterated foods on grocery store shelves, along with olive oil, milk, and orange juice. "Funny honey" can be imported or created right here at home.

Let's look at what can happen to damage a fine honey product.

CUTTING

Cutting is a processing trick committed almost exclusively in the commercial market, where huge quantities of honey—hundreds or thousands of pounds—are routinely managed. Honey is an expensive sweetener, and, when produced on a massive scale, the temptation can be strong to add any of a host of products to the bulk quantity to stretch it as far as possible but not so far that it will be rejected by the market. For instance, regular table sugar can be added to honey to correct a variety of sins. At only cents per pound, table sugar adds weight to a barrel, absorbs excess water if the honey is wet (has a moisture content above 18 percent), and masks the flavor of an unpleasant or damaged product. Sugar in honey is detectable, but until only recently it was an easy bet that the final product wouldn't be checked if it was from a reliable source, looked and tasted okay, and could be bought at an attractive price.

High-fructose corn syrup can also be added to pure honey. It, too, costs only cents per pound, and adding this cheap sweetener stretches the original amount of honey with little chance of detection. There are all manner of other sugar solutions that are equally difficult to detect. Rice fructose syrup was a common adulterant in Chinese honey for a time, and there are also dextrose, maltose, lactose, and glucose syrups.

Even water can be added to boost the moisture content of a too-dry honey to a just-right product, also adding to the amount of honey for essentially no cost to the seller. No matter the adulterant, even sophisticated detection equipment has a difficult time when the amount of adulteration is only 5 percent or less of the total amount of honey. Analysis is expensive and time consuming, and if the price is right and you don't look too hard, who's going to know or care, right?

Honey adulteration continues to be a problem for honest beekeepers who do a good job and sell a well-made product at a price they need to stay in business.

BASIC BLENDING

The value of honey can also be changed by mixing it with another honey. Honey packers, companies that buy honey from beekeepers and importers, generally have several kinds of customers, from high-end restaurants to grocery stores to large-scale bakeries and other food industries. Most honey customers aren't looking for a true varietal honey, either because they can't tell the difference or because the honey will be used in a way that makes the distinctive qualities of a varietal irrelevant. These customers want the same thing they purchased last time—usually, a medium amber, very sweet honey with just a touch of a tang at the end. To get that predictable product, honey packers blend several kinds of honeys and label the final product "Wildflower" or, commonly, "Clover."

For instance, soybean honey is often

blended with other honeys because it is inexpensive and has little flavor or color. So does adding, say, 20 percent by volume of soybean honey to a tank of clover honey constitute fraud on the part of a packer if it's marketed as clover? Clover has a distinctive flavor and color, and the addition of soybean honey hardly changes the final clover product. Technically, it's still clover honey because it's more than 50 percent clover and so meets the definition of a varietal honey. Is this a problem?

Blending honey is a legal, acceptable, and legitimate process and serves the majority of the honey-buying population just fine. Meanwhile, the artisan beekeeper has only one type of customer, honey connoisseurs who want pure varietal honeys, unique artisanal honeys, produced, harvested, processed, and handled with TLC every step of the way.

MOISTURE

Honey can be harmed by being harvested at the wrong time or by using inappropriate management techniques. There are a few ways this can happen. The first is that the honey is harvested too early.

Depending on a variety of factors, floral nectars might contain anywhere from 30 percent to 90 percent water, with a working average of about 60 percent; solids account for the rest of the nectar (though they aren't really solids when they're dissolved in nectar). After the bees have reduced the water content to about 17–18 percent, this supersaturated sugar solution has the ability to suck the water, and life, out of any bacteria, fungus, or other microscopic being that attempts to consume it. This characteristic of honey goes a long way in securing its own preservation and protection from pathogens. But when honey contains more than 20 percent water, everything changes. No longer supersaturated or able to defend itself, this uncured solution of

water and sugary nectar mixes with naturally occurring yeasts in the hive, and—voila!—you have vinegar to start with, and eventually alcohol. In fact, purposely combining the right proportions of honey, water, and the correct yeast will produce, after an appropriate amount of time, mead, the alcoholic beverage of the gods.

Unfortunately, those precise proportions seldom occur naturally, so rather than be converted to a bottle of bliss, what happens is that the hive mixture simply ferments and turns sour. The sugars fuel the yeasts that convert that sugar and water, first to acid, then alcohol, with carbon dioxide gas as a by-product. Vinegar, of course, has a distinctive, acidic, and unpleasant taste, but if it is left long enough, the mix eventually evolves into an all-alcohol product that is even more unpleasant.

Fermentation so destroys the flavor, texture, and essence of honey that proper moisture content is considered first and foremost when honey quality is in question. Fortunately, high-moisture honey is easy for beekeepers to detect using refractometers specially designed for the job. Even if fermentation has just begun, the slightest taste will be sour, and if it has advanced at all, simply opening the jar will give off a strong whiff of that musty, sour, vinegary odor that is a sure giveaway. If you have the opportunity to taste fermenting honey, you will never, ever forget it.

POOR EXTRACTING PRACTICES

Beekeepers can also ruin honey in the harvesting process by using too much honey bee repellent when separating bees from their larder, such that some of the repellent lingers. Or they can use too much smoke; a little goes a long way in a bee hive. Both of these can affect the crop the beekeeper is harvesting with a lingering and noticeable flavor.

Commercial Honey Production

Uncapping and extracting on a commercial scale are usually fairly benign activities. The harvested boxes are warmed; the wax covering the honey in the frames is removed; the honey is spun out of the frames in an extractor; and the honey is moved along to be heated, filtered, cooled, and put in industrial containers.

But from the time the honey leaves the warming room, it never stops being processed. It is pumped from the extractor to a flash heater that within seconds heats the honey to a destructive 140–170°F (depending on the equipment, the operator, and the original temperature of the honey), so that it flows rapidly through any number and kinds of filters.

You already know a bit about the chemistry of honey, so you can guess what heat will do to it. Recall the components of this sacred elixir—the sugars; the volatiles; the enzymes and proteins; the aromatics; the vitamins, minerals, and the special effects of its own terroir that give it color, aroma, and flavor—all of these attributes are stable in honey

Over the years there have been many serious issues with the quality and safety of some of the honeys that have been imported.

while it's in the hive and remain stable after the honey is removed if, and only if, it isn't heated, filtered to an extreme, or stored in a too-warm room.

This stability begins to crumble the minute the temperature of the honey increases, and this is precisely how industrial processing is vastly different from the smaller-scale operation. When the very hot honey is pumped under pressure through several filters, much, though not all, of the pollen and other microscopic particles in the honey is removed. Some material remains, which is essential because pollen is one important clue in determining the honey's type and origin, but we are essentially left with a compromised honey. Once filtered, the honey is flash cooled, down to a still destructive 120°F or so, and moved along the assembly line.

Many operations first fill a large 1,000- or even 5,000-gallon tank with the honey and routinely take samples as the tank is filling to record the moisture content and color of the honey. As more honey is added, the contents of the tank become mixed and blended to create a uniform product. When the tank is full, it's emptied into 55-gallon drums, 500-gallon plastic totes, or even tank trucks. No matter where the honey goes, however, it can be identified, because each of those containers has a

The Honey Connoisseur

Homeland Security identification number pointing directly back to that big tank, so the source, the harvest date, the beekeeper, and the color and moisture content of the honey that came from that original tank can be identified without having to open the final container.

Small-scale artisanal beekeepers tend to take much better care of their honey once it's been removed from the hive than their commercial counterparts. The goal of most small, artisanal operations is to produce a product identical to that produced by the bees, unaltered in any way by human actions. But commercial honey packers (and, yes, sometimes commercial beekeepers are also commercial packers) have very different goals. They want the honey in those jars to be radiantly clear, free from the particulate matter (dust, pollen, wax) that hastens granulation and shortens shelf life (and thus profit). And they want it to taste the same and be the same color as all the other honey on the shelves. Consistency is the name of this game.

Although an artisanal harvested honey and the industrial-scale product that most people are offered are rarely similar in appearance and characteristics, the industrial harvesting techniques, flash heating, filtering, and cooling take their toll on what was once a fine, delicate, and wonderful product.

But it could be worse. And, unfortunately, sometimes it is.

Imported Honey

As mentioned previously, the United States imports far more than half of the honey we consume, and the Department of Homeland Security has warned that one of the four most adulterated foods on U.S. grocery store shelves is honey. Over the years there have been many serious issues with the quality and safety of some of the honeys that have been imported.

Just like any other organism, the honey bee is the victim of bacterial, fungal, and viral diseases, as well as a host of micro- and macroscopic predators. One of the bacterial diseases, American foulbrood, is particularly lethal to honey bees but not people. When contracted, the disease spreads rapidly; a hive can perish in a matter of weeks if the beekeeper doesn't intervene with an antibiotic. The drugs are administered early in the spring and late in the fall, before and after the colony makes its honey crop, so as to avoid any chance of antibiotics mingling with the honey the beekeeper will eventually harvest. Production of a safe, clean product is important to honey producers and is carefully monitored by food safety inspectors in the United States at all levels.

This is where beekeepers and exporters in China (and a few other countries, as well) got into trouble several years ago. Chinese beekeepers administered antibiotic treatments at the wrong time, used treatments with a sustained life, used illegal products, or succumbed to a common medical failure: If one dose is good, two must be better. Antibiotic residues found their way into the harvested honey that those exporters were selling to the United States. At that time, shortly after the year 2000 and for a few years after that, China was selling in excess of 40 million pounds of honey to this country annually because China's government-subsidized prices were lower than prices from any other country. It took a few years, but eventually imported honey began to be scrutinized as carefully as U.S. honey, and what inspectors found was scary. An alarming amount of the honey arriving here was contaminated with detectable levels of drugs. Suddenly, honey from China and several other countries was suspect.

Contaminated honey was rejected for importation and returned to the exporter, and you might think that was the end of it. The

message seemed clear enough: Stop using illegal, ill-timed, or too much chemical product in your honey, or it will not pass muster for importation. Alas, things are seldom as simple as we would like them to be. In order to "fix" the damaged honey, the exporters subjected their product to something called "ultra-filtration," a process so radical that it took international regulators some time to catch on to what was happening.

ULTRA-FILTERED IMPORTED HONEY WORSE THAN WE THOUGHT!

To ultra-filter honey, a fair amount of water must be added to reduce its viscosity. This thinned liquid is then heated to near boiling so it can be pumped under pressure through ceramic filters with openings so fine that everything except dissolved sugar is removed—proteins, enzymes, most of the color and aroma, pollen for sure, and all those illegal drugs suspended in the solution. What comes out is nothing more than a dilute sugar solution. To reconstitute this solution to its original honey-like consistency it is immediately fast-cooled, and dehydrators reduce the water content back to about 18 percent. What remains is no longer honey but simply a syrupy sugar solution with only a tiny trace of its original chemistry.

Initially, this process wasn't fully understood by most importing countries, including the United States, and regulations defining the processed product weren't yet in place. So this honey imposter passed the existing honey test and came back into the United States at an even lower cost than the first time. To remain competitive with this extremely inexpensive imported honey U. S. Trade regulators, especially the Department of Commerce, stirred to action by an army of irate U.S. beekeepers, imposed additional tariffs on it (because it was cheap, not because it was ultra-filtered) to even out the playing field. It was a short, uneasy settlement, and it didn't last.

Trans-Shipping

The Chinese ultra-filtration hoax lasted until regulators figured out how to detect it, and Chinese beekeepers began to be less generous with their antibiotic administration. But trade barriers were still in place, so to avoid tariffs Chinese exporters sent their honey to other countries, relabeled it as originating from that second country and often gave it a varietal name, then sent it to the United States. This is a not an uncommon practice for many tariffed products being sold in the United States for less than the cost of production in their home country. It is called trans-shipping, and it enabled the honey to be sold to U.S. importers who, not surprisingly, were often front companies for complicit Chinese or other foreign honey packing companies.

Trans-shipping created a two-tier honey market in the United States. One tier comprised those who, knowingly or not, imported inexpensive honeys to unfairly compete with the other tier, composed of those who—wary of the source, the quality, and the law—would not import inexpensive honeys. Other countries, even though they were penalized with similar, though far less strict price-induced tariffs, were additionally punished by the unfair competition of the less expensive Chinese honey in the U.S. market.

Other fraudulent practices included Chinese exporters sending honey to the United States with misleading labels on the barrels, identifying the contents as a honey blend, rice sugar, or other sweetener. Once these mislabeled barrels arrived in the United States, the false labels were removed, "Pure Honey" labels applied, and the product shipped to purchasers who either unknowingly or in league with the Chinese exporters purchased an illegal product. This, too, enabled the exporters to avoid paying a tariff and contributed to the two-tier market that dominated the honey market in the

United States for more than a decade, and to some degree still does.

Combined, these practices created a grotesquely disrupted honey market not only in the United States, but across the entire globe, for years. The disruption caused by the ocean of Chinese honey flooding the U.S. market poisoned our relationship with many honey-producing countries that had previously been an integral part of the U.S. import market. Forced to find other buyers because the U.S. market was tainted, these other countries, including Argentina, Mexico, and Brazil, developed relationships throughout the world with countries that were willing to pay more for a safe and legal product.

Even by mid-2012 U.S. lawmakers had not closed all of the loopholes the Chinese honey sellers use. But as the noose has tightened on the criminal element, millions of pounds of illegal honey have been confiscated, and at least some of those organizing the fraudulent trans-shipments have been captured, put out of business, fined, deported, or imprisoned.

Reading the Label

One provision enacted during the time Chinese honey was causing such a fuss was the Country of Origin Label (COOL) law — which is still not completely in effect, so it is almost never enforced. Look at a label on a honey jar in almost any grocery store and see if you can find where the contents were produced. It might be right on the label: Product of Canada, Uruguay, Mexico, Argentina, or perhaps one of several others. Or the label might say, "Packed by" the com-

pany that sold it to the grocery store, which gives no clue where the honey originated. If you are not able to find the country of origin on the label, look on the bottle itself; often it is printed, in black, right on the neck of a plastic bottle. With an amber background it becomes nearly invisible. More often it isn't there at all. So what are they hiding, do you suppose?

Almost always the label says that the honey is U.S. Grade A—or U.S. Grade A Fancy—Pure, All Natural Honey. This has nothing to do with where it came from, but rather what the quality of the honey is, or isn't. Basically, U.S. Grade A, or even Grade A Fancy, means that the honey hasn't been damaged by too much heat, has the right moisture content, doesn't have things floating on the top, and tastes okay. It can come from the moon and still be U.S. Grade A. Curiously, many U.S. honey producers fail to acknowledge that their honey is, in fact, produced in the United States. A golden opportunity missed.

To be fair, most of the honey now entering the United States is safe, high quality, and legal. We have returned to our old trading partners, Canada, Mexico, Argentina, Brazil (which produces almost all of the world's organic honey), and several other countries. Unfortunately, trans-shipping continues from countries engaged in that illegal activity in cooperation with Chinese exporters, so vigilance and continued enforcement are required.

GMOs

There's a final blip on honey's radar screen that needs mention. The plants the bees gather nectar from have become as

much of an issue in some places as any of the problems with imported honeys. Specifically, are bees visiting GMO plants to gather nectar and make honey? Does it matter?

Briefly, GMOs (genetically modified organisms) are plants with artificially added traits that allow them to resist environmental or human-made threats—for example, toxins to resist pests or ward off viruses, herbicide-resistantance or drought-tolerance, and the like. The practice of genetic modification is most common with soybeans, field and sweet corn, sugar beets, cotton, alfalfa, canola, rice, squash, potatoes, radish, and flax. Undoubtedly, more plants are under study as potential subjects.

When it comes to honey and GMO plants the issues get murky. One camp believes that food from GMO crops should be labeled, so everyone knows what they are eating, and any food product that is raised on GMO food—think beef cows eating GMO alfalfa—should also be labeled, according to this camp. The other camp is convinced that GMO crops are the answer to world food production because they cost less to produce, require fewer protective chemical applications, yield more per acre, and allow some crops to grow where they have never grown before. The truth is that when government-supported industrial agriculture comes head to head with fanatical citizen resistance it's not as easy being green as you'd like, no matter which side you choose. The European Union and the United Kingdom have been more resistant to GMO

agriculture than the United States, with its 70-plus million acres of GMO crops. The EU and the UK both have restrictions on growing GMO crops and require serious label warnings on GMO food products not grown but sold there; both have a general disregard for moving in the direction of GMOs in the immediate future.

It quickly became clear that imported honey derived from GMO plants contained pollen from those plants. The honey was at first banned altogether, but eventually a compromise was reached and a label settled upon that says, "Contains Pollen From GMO Plants." And, for a product to be called honey it must contain pollen, at least there, and perhaps even here, as the definition of honey with, or without pollen is still in the courts.

With the new GMO labeling in early 2012 came yet another change in the global honey market. Suddenly, honey from Argentina and many other non-European countries that had been welcome in the UK and EU because of its quality (compared to Chinese and trans-shipped honey) was no longer viable there because it

contained GMO pollen. But right about then the door closed on Chinese honey in the United States due to even tighter tariff restrictions and inspections, so China had honey to spare. The solution seemed simple. Excess Chinese honey (much more acceptable now that it had been cleaned up to meet U.S. demands) found a home in Europe and much of Asia, while those GMO honey crops have found a home, again, in U.S. markets.

The U.S. Department of Agriculture has been reluctant to let any crops have discriminatory labels. For instance, milk can't be labeled as not containing hormones, soybeans can't be labeled as not being GMOs, and it cannot be said that cotton seed oil is GMO, or not. The USDA is reluctant to give consumers a choice because it is convinced that there is no difference between such products relative to health or safety. That philosophy seems to dominate all of the food labeling requirements in the United States lately, and it appears that it won't change in the near future. However, the case hasn't rested, and individual states are beginning to challenge these restrictions. Not surprisingly, the companies that produce the GMO plants and the products that use them are reluctant to give in. Certainly, the attorneys and the media benefit from the controversy. The final vote has yet to be cast.

Honey has been lucky. Even though it has often been abused, it is not generally thought of as a diminished product. Recall the Alar scare with apples, the herbicide issue surrounding cranberries some time ago, and the pink slime brouhaha more recently. Entire industries have been decimated because of rumor rather than actual danger. What has been damaged in the honey market, however, is the ability of the United States to produce its own honey. We depend on the kindness of strangers for much of this sublime sweetener. That is the biggest crime of all.

Honey has been lucky. Even though it has often been abused, it is not generally thought of as a diminished product.

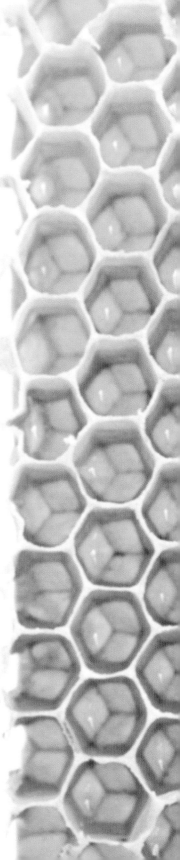

CHAPTER }5

TASTING HONEY

We have learned that several factors can elevate a good-tasting honey to a great-tasting honey. Those factors can include a field of abundant, nectar-rich flowers, the local terroir, and the hand of an experienced beekeeper. But, when we describe the taste of honey, we are referring to more than just its sweetness; we are referring to a fullness of flavor. Honey, like sugar, is sweet but what sets it apart is flavor. Great honey has layers of flavor that cannot be found in any other sweetener.

Grassy, earthy, floral, and metallic are just some of the flavor notes you will encounter when tasting honey. Becoming a discerning honey taster means educating your palate and learning to identify the individual flavors that burst forth in each spoonful. At the same time, it is important to remember that preference for flavor is entirely subjective, so what you ultimately consider to be a great-tasting honey is one that you enjoy. Our goal is not to suggest that some honeys taste better than others; it is to help you learn to identify and appreciate the flavor of every honey you taste.

Honey tasting begins with any jar of good-quality honey from your local farmer's market, gourmet or specialty food store, or better grocery store. There are also many interesting selections online to choose from. Begin by reading the label. If included, note the name of the floral source, the location in which the honey was produced, and even the producer's name. This information will give you clues as to what you might expect to taste.

After consulting the label, lift the jar to the light to observe the color of the honey. Clover honey, for example, falls in the light to medium amber family with pale straw

Tasting Honey

to golden yellow hues, depending on how much of it is actually derived from clover nectar. If it's darker, there's likely another nectar source mixed in. Take a closer look at the honey and decide whether it is transparent or cloudy. Most good-quality honey is cloudy, because it still has all of its natural pollen. Some honeys, like black locust and fireweed, are naturally transparent; so perfectly transparent honeys have not necessarily been commercially processed.

Unscrew the jar and take a few good, deep sniffs to catch the aroma. Think about what you smell. You might immediately recognize the warm aroma of beeswax, earthy pollen, or pungent yeast. These are aromas naturally found in honey and will vary in presence and strength depending on each sample. Again, with a clover honey, for example, you should also smell the distinct aroma of dry grass. Do you detect any other aromas? A hint of spiciness reminiscent of cinnamon is also common in clover honey.

Now, with a clean spoon, scoop up a generous amount of honey, spread it on your tongue and let it melt slowly until it covers your entire tongue. Close your mouth, but don't

swallow yet. You may detect an initial sweetness. As the honey sits on your tongue, notice its texture. Some honeys are creamy, while others are buttery or coarse. Continue to let the honey melt on your tongue and become the same temperature as your body. Now inhale through your mouth and exhale through your nose. As the aromas reach the olfactory glands in your nasal cavity, the flavors come into focus. Concentrate on each flavor and when it appears during the tasting process. Note whether it is mild or assertive. How long does it last? Now swallow the honey. A slight burn at the back of your throat usually means there is a good amount of pollen in the sample. Always expect a certain amount of pollen in your honey as a sign that it's been minimally processed.

The best way to learn to recognize the flavors and subtleties of honey is to taste different ones side by side. Following these basic steps allows you to engage all of your senses to evaluate the flavor profile and floral source of each honey. There are thousands of flavors found in honey, and the first step to tasting them is to train your senses to tease them out. The next step is to distinguish between the flavors and describe them clearly.

The Sensory Analysis of Honey

As honey establishes its place in the culinary world, its future lies in the recognition and appreciation of the wide variety of flavor profiles and the many wonderful ways these flavors can pair with and enhance the taste of other foods. Sensory analysis is the intimate exploration and appraisal of a food, beverage—in this case, honey—by engaging all the senses to determine what flavors are present, their intensities, and the order of their appearances during the tasting process. It is also used to detect negative attributes when a honey has an off flavor or is fermented. With a little practice and our honey-tasting guide, you will cultivate your palate and gradually learn how to recognize a good-quality honey and identify its floral sources by color, aroma, and flavor.

We provide useful tools, including a honey color chart, a honey tasting wheel with a glossary of words to describe the aromas and flavors you experience, and a tasting scorecard so you can keep track of your experiences as you taste. It's always a good idea to take notes during the tasting process. Your notes will help you to memorize the honeys and flavors you've tasted, thus developing your palate, and will later serve as a handy reminder of the qualities you discovered in each honey. The subtle flavors might be difficult to distinguish in the beginning, but once you become acquainted with the tasting process and terminology, it won't be long before your palate evolves and you master the skills of honey tasting.

Let's Get Started

Gather some jars of honey and read the following paragraphs to learn more about applying sensory analysis techniques to tasting honey. You'll need the following items to begin:

- 6 different varietals of honey
- transparent or white glass cups, preferably bowl shaped
- teaspoons for tasting and stirring
- Honey Connoisseur Color Guide
- Honey Connoisseur Aroma and Tasting Wheel
- Honey Connoisseur Tasting Scorecard and a pencil*
- water, at room temperature
- freshly-sliced green apple or bread
- napkins

Use the honey tasting scorecard to record your observations and impressions as you taste each honey. In the first column, write in the name of each honey you will taste. Follow our guidelines for assessing color, aroma, flavor and texture then write your notes in the designated column. Use the honey color chart and aroma and tasting wheel to help you identify your impressions.

Establishing Your Tasting Environment

It is advisable not to smoke; drink or eat; brush your teeth; or apply perfume or scented aftershave, soap, or shampoo directly before a tasting. The tastes and aromas will linger on your tongue or body and confuse your senses, making it difficult to accurately evaluate the flavor of each honey.

The best time to taste is early in the morning before eating anything, when your taste buds are fresh and wide awake. Water or freshly-sliced green apples are the best palate cleansers to use between tasting different honeys. The water should be room temperature, never ice cold, since cold water will make your mouth cold and prevent the honey from gently melting on your tongue. It will also dull your taste buds. You can nibble on the apple or bread between tastes to clear your palate so you will be able to clearly taste the next honey. Taste no more than six different honeys at each sitting and pause for two or three minutes after each, or you risk overexposing your senses and experiencing what professional tasters call a collapsed palate. In order to combat olfactory fatigue, you can reset your sensitivity by smelling freshly ground coffee beans. This will work a few times, but eventually you will have to take a break and completely rest your nose. Tasting honey with a slight cold or stuffy nose will make it more difficult to recognize flavors, and every honey may simply taste sweet.

Presenting the Honeys

It is estimated that 80 percent of the information that comes to our brain is from visual stimuli. We all form opinions of products by their visual appearance, the packaging and labels. Fancy or unusual packaging can be distracting or sway a taster's judgment. In the end, the quality and flavor of the honey will prevail, but first impressions do count, so the honey you taste should be presented in unadorned glass containers similar in size and shape; this serves to keep all samples equal and anonymous. Transparent glasses with a wide mouth are recommended. This allows you to get your nose deep in the bowl to smell the honey and also to observe its color and all of its

marvelous visual qualities.

Write down the name of each honey on a small piece of paper and set it next to each glass. It is also helpful to number each sample, so it can be easily identified on the Honey-Tasting Scorecard. For a completely blind tasting, present the honeys in dark-colored glasses to conceal the colors and label each sample only with a number. This kind of tasting is to concentrate on identifying only flavor profiles; later you may evaluate color and textures.

COLOR

Color is the first clue to identifying a honey and an important indicator of its botanical origin. Spotted knapweed honey is always light, tulip poplar is extremely dark, and gallberry is a shade of amber. Each varietal of honey generally falls within a color range, with slight variations depending on the vintage and terroir. You might think that all light honeys are mild and dark honeys are heavy and rich, but you will be surprised to learn that the color does not always correspond with what we expect to taste.

All colors change when viewed in different light, so natural, evenly cast sunlight, rather than indoor artificial light, is best for assessing color; but whatever lighting source you have available, be consistent and use it to assess all honey samples.

Hold the honey sample up to a window and let the sun shine through it. Then look at the honey against a white surface, away from other colors and objects.

The HONEY CONNOISSEUR COLOR GUIDE

There are seven designated colors of honey in varying intensities from water white to dark amber. This standard system for measuring the color of liquid honey is called the Pfund color grading system. Color is measured visually using a glass tile and is expressed as the relative lightness or darkness of amber on a scale in millimeters. Below are the seven colors of honey using the Pfund system and a few types of varietal honeys that correspond to those colors.

CREAM – PEARL – BLUSH – BEIGE – LIGHT CHARTREUSE – STRAW – BANANA

| 0 MM | WATER WHITE | 8 MM |

BUTTER – MAIZE – CITRUS – GREEN

| 8 MM | EXTRA WHITE | 17 MM |

YELLOW – MARIGOLD – BUTTERSCOTCH – SUNFLOWER – DAFFODIL – BRASS

| 17 MM | WHITE | 34 MM |

APRICOT – CORAL – SALMON – PEACH – DUSTY – PUMPKIN – ORANGE

| 34 MM | EXTRA LIGHT AMBER | 50 MM |

MANGO – CLEMENTINE – FLAME – BURNT ORANGE – AUBURN – BRICK

| 50 MM | LIGHT AMBER | 85 MM |

BLOOD – MAROON – CLARET – PLUM – MAHOGANY – RAWHIDE – CAROB – HENNA

| 85 MM | AMBER | 114 MM |

CLOVE – COCOA – EARTH – MINERAL – HAZELNUT

| 114 MM | DARK AMBER | 140 MM |

Honey is extremely rich in color beyond the seven shades of ambers represented by the Pfund color chart. Our color chart also includes a spectrum of other colors you may observe in your honey samples.

Colors also change depending on the context in which they are viewed, including the other colors around it. Now consult the Honey Color Chart to decide what color your honey is.

The Pfund color chart is a basic tool to assess the color of honey, but honey is extremely rich in color beyond the seven shades of ambers represented there. Our Honey Color Guide, is a spectrum of other colors that you may observe in your honey samples.

Once you've established the color of your honey, record your description in the second column of your Honey Tasting Scorecard.

CLARITY AND CONSISTENCY

Next observe whether the honey is transparent, cloudy, or opaque and note your observation in the second column of your Honey Tasting Scorecard. Good-quality honey is rarely 100 percent transparent, nor should it be. There will often be a bit of cloudiness, depending on the amount of beeswax, pollen, or dust that is naturally present. Most beekeepers use light straining to remove particles like bee parts, wax, or stray wood pieces from the hive. Still, the honey should be slightly murky. Commercially made honey is often absolutely transparent because of the type of filter process that's used. Do you notice any other impurities besides the normal pollen or occasional piece of beeswax?

Observe and take note of the honey's

HERE ARE A FEW EXAMPLES OF WAYS TO DESCRIBE THE COLOR *of* VARIOUS HONEYS.

Water white with creamy gold: *black locust, fireweed)*

Extra white with greenish and pale beige tones: *tupelo, linden*

Extra light amber with apricot orange hues: *sourwood, orange blossom*

Light amber with pale butter and light beige tones: *acacia*

Dark amber with deep reddish tints: *Japanese knotweed, chestnut*

Dark amber with purple tints: *heather, tulip poplar*

consistency. Some honeys crystallize, and others never do. Tupelo, acacia, and black sage honeys, for example, are known never to crystallize unless other nectar sources blooming in the region at the same time have mixed with the honey. Crystallization is a natural process in which liquid honey turns solid as the water evaporates, forming granular crystals. Liquid honey that has become solid through crystallization turns completely opaque and lighter in color. If the honey has crystallized, are the granules consistently and evenly layered or swirled? Take note of the size of the granules: Are they small or large? Smaller crystals make for a delightfully smooth mouth feel. Large, coarse granules are undesirable and unpleasant. If you find extremely large and crude crystals in your honey or crystallization in odd patterns around the side of the jar, it could mean the honey was overheated or adulterated. We will discuss tasting crystallized honey in more detail. Has the honey separated into solid and liquid? This could be a sign that it has fermented. The aroma and taste will confirm this.

AROMA

Of all our senses, the olfactory is the most powerful. Smell is a chemical sense that is transported by molecules, and humans can perceive hundreds of thousands of aromas.

SCORECARD

Honey Connoisseur Tasting

HONEY	COLOR	AROMA	FLAVOR	TEXTURE

It is our most memorable sense, yet there are people who, for genetic reasons, have aromatic blind spots and simply cannot experience certain aromas.

Aromas can profoundly affect our emotions, and some can ignite vivid memories. We often associate smells with people, places, or things, and those associations become permanent scent memories. We can call upon this built-in aroma database to both distinguish and name aromas and flavors when tasting honey. Neurophysiologists tell us that our perception of taste is 90 percent smell and only 10 percent taste; so when we talk about tasting, we must take smell into account.

The best way to capture the full aroma of honey is at ambient temperatures. Heat and humidity increase the movement of the molecules in honey making it much easier to smell. Cup the bowl of honey in the palm of one hand for a minute or two until it warms up. Then tilt and swirl the honey around the inside of the tasting glass. By increasing its surface area, you expose a larger portion of the honey to the olfactory receptors in your nose. Use your other hand to cup the top of the bowl for a moment to trap the aromas inside. Then remove your hand, dip your nose into the bowl, and take a few deep, short sniffs to get a good dose of the aroma.

This is not the time to take a polite sniff; get your nose as close to the honey as possible. Move the honey away from your nose for a moment, and then sniff it again; repeat this. By waving the honey under your nose and taking short sniffs, you maximize the scent impressions you take in. Since our sense of smell fatigues within six seconds, it is important to concentrate and try to identify the aromas quickly.

Notice the intensity and quality of the aromas. Ask yourself, Are the aromas strong or weak? Are they abrupt, or do they linger? Using the numbers 0–4, note the intensity of the aroma on your Honey Tasting Scorecard in the third column.

0 = No aroma
1 = Weak aroma
2 = Medium aroma
3 = Strong aroma
4 = Very strong aroma

You may find that these aromas don't always match up with what you'll taste later.

Are you able to identify what aromas you smell? It might be easier to ask yourself what the aroma reminds you of. Aromas are based upon a honey's predominant floral source. Using the Honey Aroma and Tasting Wheel, try to assign the aroma of

---

HERE ARE EXAMPLES OF AROMA FAMILIES AND A FEW *of* THE HONEYS COMMONLY ASSOCIATED WITH THEM.

Floral: *goldenrod, tupelo, tulip poplar*

Fruit: *blueberry, blackberry, orange*

Warm: *guajillo, cat's claw, fireweed*

Animal: *leatherwood, ulmo*

Woody: *manuka, heather, chestnut, tamarisk*

Fresh: *lavender, thyme, mint*

Chemical: *fireweed, spotted knapweed*

Spoiled: *tamarisk, apple blossom, black locust, sage*

Vegetal: *clover, alfalfa, linden*

the honey to the aroma family that best describes what you smell. The nine aroma families are found on the innermost circle of the tasting wheel and include floral, fruit, warm, animal, woody, fresh, chemical, spoiled, and vegetal. On the outside of the wheel are more specific terms to describe the aromas. A group of aromas is referred to as a bouquet. If you can smell more than one aroma in a honey, try to identify each one and decide which is most prominent. There is no right or wrong—only your own impressions matter—but your scent memory will improve with practice.

VISCOSITY AND TEXTURE

The viscosity and texture of honey are integral parts of the tasting experience and, although less influential than aroma, partly responsible for how we perceive flavor. Viscosity can be described as the honey's body or simply its weight on your tongue. Texture, on the other hand, is the tactile quality of a honey in your mouth, referred to as *mouth feel*. Keep in mind that when tasting honey, temperature and humidity can dramatically change both of these impressions, as well as aroma. Warm honey coats the tongue like a blanket and reveals all of its qualities up front. Cold honey delivers an unpleasant shock to the tongue before finally melting, therefore delaying the delivery of its sensory qualities.

Begin to perceive the viscosity and texture of the honey while swirling it around in the bowl. Notice the speed at which it moves around the glass. That is the first clue to assessing the honey's viscosity, or weight. Think about the weight of the honey as it sits on your tongue and slides down your throat. Its weight in your mouth depends on its water-to-sugar ratio. Honeys produced in dryer climates or close to the equator tend to be

Recognizing Fermentation

OR BURNED OR OFF FLAVORS IN HONEY

Fermentation occurs in a honey that has a moisture content greater than 17–18 percent, at which point the delicate balance of sugars is upset and provides favorable conditions for the growth of yeast. The aroma of fermenting honey—associated with fermented beverages like mead and sweet wine or fermenting fruit or bread—is easily recognized. If you taste fermented honey, you will experience a mild tingling sensation in your mouth.

The fresh nectar collected by bees is high in moisture content. Until it is completely cured and ripened by the bees, then capped over, it should not be harvested by the beekeeper. If the honey is extracted too soon, it could ferment quickly, making for an unpleasant tasting experience. Honey should ideally be stored in dry, cool places. This will reduce the chance of fermenting.

Dark honeys that have lost their fresh flavors, with the distinctive taste of caramel, may have been overheated or otherwise improperly stored. Smoky flavors can end up in your honey if bee keepers use too much smoke on their colonies when removing bees from the honey supers or overheat or scorch the honey when bottling. The smell and flavor of overly smoky or burned honey are unpleasant and can overpower the delicate honey flavors. Some honeys, like avocado and tamarisk, naturally have a smoky aroma and flavor.

Some honeys crystallize naturally, while others can be initiated by the beekeeper to crystallize. No matter the origin, crystallization gives honey a thick, spreadable texture and lighter color than its liquid counterpart. Tiny particles floating in the air, such as dust, pollen, and air bubbles, settle inside honey and act as nuclei that form crystals. This happens rather quickly in honeys with more than 30 percent glucose (dextrose). When the temperature of honey goes down to between 60°F and 75°F, the crystals grow rapidly, forming small textured crystals, which are characteristic of finely granulated honeys that feel smooth on your tongue. Crystals that form below 60°F or above 75°F, grow slowly and form large, sharp crystals giving those honeys a coarse, gritty, and unpleasant texture.

The size and quality of the crystals make the difference between a luscious, smooth-textured honey and one with an undesirable, gritty mouth feel. Pay special attention to these impressions when tasting honeys that are granulated. Use a spoon to stir your crystallized honey so you can see the size and shape of its granules. Ideally, you should not see any large, coarse crystals, but if you do they should be smaller than fine sand. Scoop a dollop of honey onto your tongue, close your mouth, and sandwich the honey between your tongue and the roof of your mouth. As it warms, feel the texture of the granules on your tongue. Take note of the size and texture of the granules; they may be creamy, fine, smooth, sawdusty, sandy, or gritty. The smaller the crystals, the smoother the texture will be. You are looking for an overall mouth feel that is pleasant and smooth and crystals that are uniform and fine throughout. Let the honey sit on your tongue for a moment and allow it to gradually dissolve from the heat of

thicker and have a fuller body with a lower moisture content. Try to determine whether the honey feels thin like water, medium bodied like a milk shake, or full bodied like yogurt. The weight of the honey does not necessarily reflect its quality or final flavor.

To determine the honey's texture, roll it around your mouth, feel it between your tongue and palate, then imagine what kind of food or fabric it might be compared to. Use descriptive words like buttery, silky, velvety, grippy, jammy, or felted. Avocado and blueberry honeys have a smooth, buttery texture like silk, while the desert honeys such as mesquite, tamarisk, and guajillo tend to be thick and velvety. Kiawe is full bodied with an absolutely silky texture but a suede-like viscosity. Fireweed honey might be described as full bodied and grippy, buckwheat honey as medium bodied with a texture like chamois.

Make a note of the viscosity and texture in the fifth column of your Honey Tasting Scorecard.

your mouth. The delicate granules should gradually soften and vanish on your tongue, making for a sumptuous experience. During the process, if you feel granules that are offensive or have the sensation of rock candy, you may want to gently liquefy the jar of honey, using a controlled heat source to melt those harsh crystals. Some people may prefer to leave the larger crystals, however, and spread the chunky honey on bread. The choice is yours.

You might come across a honey that appears to have separated into two layers. At the bottom of the jar will be a solid, granulated mass of honey, and floating on top of that will be a separate layer of liquid honey. This usually occurs in crystallized honeys that have been stored in too warm temperatures. The sugar crystals have separated from the water and begun to ferment. This is also a sign of aging honey. Unfortunately, this defect cannot be corrected and is generally considered unacceptable by consumers.

Some honeys exist naturally in a gel-like consistency. When they are mixed or shaken, they change consistency and become a liquid. When they are left alone, they return to their gel-like state. This unique property is called thixotropy, and few honeys claim it. Thixotropic honeys are not considered crystallized; they just have thicker body than liquid honeys and can be compared to jelly. Ling heather honey from Scotland is the most famous thixotropic honey, while manuka from New Zealand and karvy honey from India also are known to exhibit this quality. If you have the good fortune to get hold of one of these honeys, try stirring it, and watch it turn to liquid and back to jelly again. Take a spoonful and examine the texture on your tongue. The mouth feel can be described as chewy or velvety, even scratchy, until the honey melts away completely.

Taste and Flavor

Taste and flavor are often used interchangeably, but, in fact, their perception relies on two different sensory systems. Our ability to taste is actually quite limited. The taste bud receptors on the human tongue can distinguish only five basic taste sensations, but we are able to taste thousands of different flavors. Sweet, sour, salty, bitter, and umami are the taste sensations we experience on our tongue when food, including honey is mixed with our own saliva. The impressions we perceive as flavor are really aromas moving from the back of the throat up to the nose and into the retro-nasal passage where

What Kind of Taster Are You?

Scientists use sensitivity to bitterness to define an individual's innate level of tasting. If you are highly sensitive to bitter foods, you are considered a taster and referred to as a super taster. If you can tolerate bitterness, you are considered a non-taster. Although super tasters are keen tasters, that does not necessarily make them better tasters. Tasting is all about the ability to identify aromas, textures, and flavors and then effectively communicate those observations. It is possible for both types of taster, super and non, and those in between, to become savvy honey tasters with a little bit of practice.

The History of
Sensory Analysis of Honey

Dr. Eva Crane, a British researcher and author, was one of the first people to write extensively about bees and honey. In 1942, during World War II, when sugar was difficult to obtain, Eva and her husband, James, received a beehive as a wedding present. That hive would become a source of sweet honey and would fuel her lifelong fascination with beekeeping. She dedicated her entire life to gathering valuable information about apiculture while traveling to over sixty often primitive countries. Dr. Crane founded the International Bee Research Association (IBRA) and wrote close to two hundred papers and articles about bees and honey. Her books *Honey: A Comprehensive Survey* (1975) and *The World History of Beekeeping and Honey Hunting* (1999) were groundbreaking tomes chock full of information about every aspect of beekeeping, information that could be found nowhere else. Although Crane's books are still one of the best sources for information about honey, she did not address the sensory aspects of honey or provide details about flavor profiles. She briefly touched on the compounds responsible for the aromas and flavors of honey and identified many by name, but she remained one step from linking them to sensory analysis.

During the 1960s, Dr. Jonathan White Jr. wrote over 140 articles for the United States Department of Agriculture (USDA) about all aspects of honey, including its chemistry and adulteration. In one paper, White discussed the effects of area of production on the composition of honey, briefly referring to terroir, and in another he noted the relationship of honey color to its composition. In his sixty-year career of research and investigation, White accumulated the largest body of written work on honey in the United States; however, he, too, just touched on the sensory analysis of tasting honeys and terroir.

It wasn't until the 1970s that a French team of expert tasters led by Michel Gonnet and Gabriel Vache began to adapt sensory analysis techniques for tasting honey. Gonnet set the standards by writing the first formal honey-tasting curriculum for the International Honey Commission (IHC), which was established in 1979 under the umbrella of Apimondia, an international federation of beekeepers that promotes apiculture. These first sensory methods for tasting honey were based on the protocol and experience learned in the olive oil industry. Gonnet recommended that all beekeepers should be trained in these sensory techniques in order to better understand the honey they were harvesting and marketing. Unfortunately, the IHC has disbanded, but Apimondia still holds biennial conferences with educational lectures about bees and honey.

Michel Gonnet was a pioneer who paved the way for the growing interest in tasting honey and its sensory analysis. Today, the Italian National Register of Experts in the Sensory Analysis of Honey borrows Gonnet's techniques and uses them in training courses to teach others how to apply the sensory analysis of important unifloral honeys of Italy. These courses include training in the sensory analysis of honey and all other aspects of beekeeping and honey plants. Expert Italian honey tasters are known as honey ambassadors (*ambasciatori del miele*; AMI) and are expert beekeepers as well.

we perceive aroma. When we are exposed to any of the five basic taste sensations combined with aroma and texture, we perceive the total experience as flavor.

TASTE

Humans have thousands of taste buds inside those tiny bumps on the tongue, which are called *papillae*. Taste buds are found not only on the tongue, but also on the roof of the mouth and in the throat; surprisingly, the center of the tongue is somewhat taste blind. The taste receptors we call taste buds send messages to the brain that tell us which taste we are experiencing.

Sweetness is the most common taste associated with honey, but as you sample different types of honeys, you will discover that some taste sweeter than others. A honey's sweetness depends on the composition of its sugars and on the nectar source. Honeys with higher portions of glucose to fructose tend to taste overly sweet. Raspberry and fireweed honeys are relatively sweeter than chestnut and sage honeys. You probably will be surprised to discover that not all honeys are sweet. Some can be interpreted as quite bitter, sharp, or pungent. Honeys that are said to taste bitter are chestnut, avocado, tamarisk, and heather honeys. All honeys are fairly acidic, imparting tartness or sourness, but their high sugar content masks that bitterness more often than not. Cranberry and apple blossom honeys have a pleasant tart quality about them that makes them stand out

Saltiness is not a taste one would normally associate with honey, but it can be detected in those honeys produced from botanical sources with origins close to the shore of any major seacoast. For example, it is possible to taste the saltiness of the ocean in saw palmetto and black mangrove honeys from Florida's coast.

Honey is also rarely described as having the taste of umami, or savory, yet tamarisk has a savory soy-like flavor note. Although neither salty nor umami is a taste normally considered characteristic of honey, pairing honey with salty foods like cheeses can deeply enhance the honey's flavors. We'll learn more about that in chapter 6.

FLAVOR

Try this short exercise to appreciate the difference between taste and flavor. Pinch your nose to shut off your nasal passage, then take a spoonful of honey and spread it on your tongue. Let the honey sit on your tongue and melt. Concentrate and try to describe what you taste. You should only be able to taste a sweet liquid that you might not even recognize as honey. This is the taste part of the exercise. Now unpinch your nose to open your nasal passage, inhale from your mouth, and breathe naturally, exhaling from your nose. You should suddenly experience an explosion of flavors, analogous to someone coming into a dark room and switching on the light. The flavors that you now "taste" are actually aromas moving from your mouth to your nose. These are called retro-nasal aromas. When the aroma of the honey circulates between your nose

Beeswax, Pollen, and Propolis

To truly know and understand the flavors of honey, it is essential to be familiar with the sensory qualities of beeswax, bee pollen, and propolis, because they are all found inside the beehive and will end up in the honey during harvesting.

The aroma of beeswax can be described as warm, sweet, and reminiscent of honey, depending on its quality. The beeswax cells are where honey bees store bee pollen, which also takes on a variety of sensory qualities depending on the type of flower it was gathered from. Bee pollen has a distinctive sweet, nutty, often earthy flavor, resembling that of herba-ceous flowers. A large quantity of bee pollen in honey is associated with the throat-catching sensation or slight sting that's sometimes felt when swallowing honey. The burn can be attributed to the antibacterial properties found in honey.

Propolis is the taffy-like glue created by honey bees from the sap of various trees. It is highly aromatic, with notes of resin, beeswax, and turpentine. Propolis is used to seal cracks inside the hive to deter pests and bacteria in preparation for the upcoming winter season. Honey bees occasionally store small balls of propolis inside the wax cells, and they often end up in the honey.

and mouth, the olfactory receptors in your nasal cavity detect them and communicate to your brain what you perceive as flavor. This happens in two stages, first when we inhale and more significantly when we exhale.

Now let's taste honey, this time concentrating on the flavors. Scoop up another generous spoonful of honey, coat your entire tongue, let it melt slowly and savor the flavors as they unfold. Take your time. It is important to distribute a generous amount of honey on your tongue and throughout your mouth to fully taste and acknowledge the flavors. Inhale through your mouth and exhale through your nose. As the aromas travel to your nose, you might experience flavors that are fruity, vegetal, fresh, or animal. You might detect more specific flavors, like apricot, green bananas, or what you imagine dry hay would taste like. There are thousands of different flavors, called notes, found in honey, and we continue to perceive them even after we swallow.

HONEY AROMA AND TASTING WHEEL

Often the flavors we taste in a honey are not consistent with the aromas we perceive when we smell the honey in the jar or bowl. Refer to the Honey Aroma and Tasting Wheel and use it as a guide to describe the flavors; then record them in the fourth column of your Honey Tasting Scorecard.

Begin in the center of the wheel and decide which of the nine flavor families best identifies your honey sample; there might be one or more adjectives for each. Once you decide on the flavor family, you can work your way to the outside of the wheel, becoming more and more specific with the words you use to describe what you taste.

For example, working from the center of the wheel, orange blossom honey can initially be described as floral and fruity. As you move toward the outside of the wheel, you may decide that the predominant flavor is fruity. As you reach the outer edge of the wheel, you are prompted to think about whether you detect any other subtle flavors, such as orange, prune, apple, apricot, or any combination thereof.

In turn, mesquite honey could initially be described as having warm desert notes with hints of caramel, toffee, or brown sugar. Pay attention to the intensity and clarity of the flavors you discover. More often than not, the flavors you encounter will be found on the wheel, but should you come across some that are not, you should be able to pinpoint the general families they fall into and then free associate to come up with your own descriptions. Sometimes you may need to make up a few colorful words to describe a

Honey Connoisseur
Aroma *and* Tasting Wheel

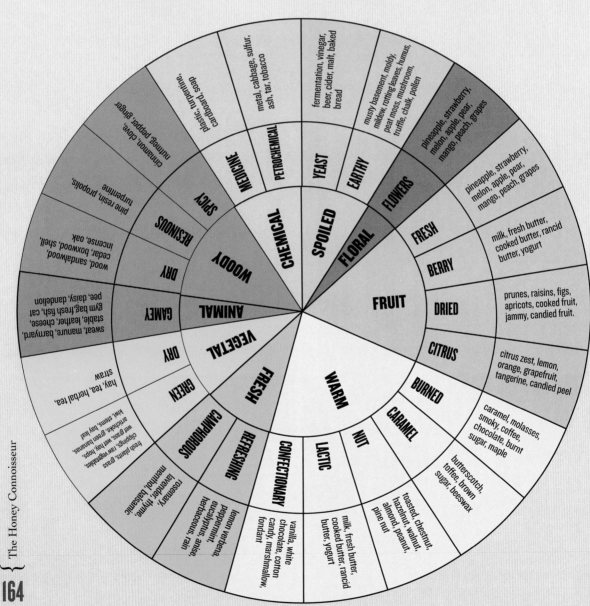

flavor or use adjectives that fall outside of the original flavor family; the tasting process is fluid and sometimes throws us some surprises. Get creative!

As you taste, concentrate on when the flavor notes show up and whether they are weak or assertive. Which flavors make themselves known right away, and which show up after a few seconds of the honey being on your tongue? The finish, or end, is another word for the aftertaste. Do the flavors persist or do they end abruptly.

Tulip poplar honey, for example, reveals its floral flavor notes up front; as it melts on your tongue, you will perceive a raisin and dried fruit flavor in the middle that lingers until the finish. Apple blossom honey is very fruity up front, with a crispy, cider finish. Linden honey begins quite sweet; then you taste dried apricots and end with a slightly bitter green melon finish. Outstanding honeys have flavors that linger on your palate for twenty seconds or longer.

Taste each honey again to see if you notice any new flavors or any difference in the timing of their appearance. Sometimes it takes a few tastes before you will notice the subtle distinctions. Take note of what new qualities you discover with each spoonful. As you taste, think about what types of foods might complement that honey. When people ask me what my favorite honey is, my answer is that it depends on what I'm eating with it. Pairing honeys with other foods is how most of us will enjoy them. Pairing is also where the notes you made on your tasting card will come in handy.

If you concentrate and use the sensory analysis techniques you have learned here to describe each flavor as specifically as possible, your chances of remembering and identifying that honey again in the future increases. Use the tasting terminology each time you taste to increase your understanding and memory of what you taste. With practice you can become an accomplished taster, by simply concentrating when you taste and memorizing the tasting vocabulary. Review your tasting notes periodically and decide which characteristics you enjoyed the most and the least. Your tasting notes become your own personal sensory vocabulary. In the end you are educating your palate so you can select honeys that you enjoy and that will complement your food.

Glossary *of* Honey Tasting Terms

This following list contains words specially related to the aromas and flavors you will find when tasting honey. There are nine general families listed in bold capital letters that relate to the overall impression for each honey. Each family is subdivided into more specific words and examples of foods that will help you better increase your ability to describe what you taste.

FLORAL

FLOWERS: violet, rose, geranium, peony, hyacinth, honeysuckle, jasmine

FRUIT

FRESH: pineapple, strawberry, melon, apple, pear, mango, peach, grape

BERRY: blackcurrant, raspberry, blackberry, cherry, cranberry

DRIED: prune, raisin, fig, apricot, cooked fruit, jammy, candied fruit

CITRUS: citrus zest, lemon, orange, grapefruit, tangerine, candied peel

WARM

BURNED: caramel, molasses, smoky, coffee, chocolate, burnt sugar, maple

CARAMEL: butterscotch, toffee, brown sugar, beeswax

NUT: toasted, chestnut, hazelnut, walnut, almond, peanut, pine nut

LACTIC: milk, fresh butter, cooked butter, rancid butter, yogurt

CONFECTIONARY: vanilla, white chocolate, cotton candy, marshmallow, fondant

FRESH

VEGETAL

GREEN: fresh plants, raw vegetables, wet grass, wet hay, hops, artichoke, green bananas, kiwi, bay leaf

DRY: hay, tea, herbal tea, straw

REFRESHING: lemon verbena, peppermint, eucalyptus, anise, herbaceous, rain

CAMPHOROUS: rosemary, lavender, thyme, menthol, balsamic

ANIMAL

GAMEY: sweat, manure, barnyard, stable, leather, cheese, gym bag, fresh fish, cat urine, daisy, dandelion

WOODY

DRY: wood, sandalwood, cedar, boxwood, shells, incense, oak

RESINOUS: pine resin, propolis, turpentine

SPICY: cinnamon, clove, nutmeg, pepper, ginger

CHEMICAL

MEDICINE: plastic, turpentine, cardboard, soap

PETRO-CHEMICAL: metal, cabbage, sulfur, ash, tar, tobacco

SPOILED

YEAST: fermentation, vinegar, beer, cider, malt, baked bread, dough

EARTHY: musty basement, moldy, mildew, rotting leaves, humus, peat moss, mushroom, truffle, chalk, pollen

Planning a Honey Tasting Party

Hosting your own honey tasting party is a festive way to entertain friends and family while learning about different types of honey and their flavors. All you need are some jars of honey, enough spoons for each guest to taste each honey, good company, and an open mind. You can organize your tasting by deciding to serve only local honeys or international or single-source honeys. You can even throw a potluck tasting and ask each guest to bring a honey. No matter what type of party you choose to throw, think about offering a wide variety of honeys. The variety could include various colors, plant sources, and terroir. Try to include one very unusual or surprising honey. You may opt to host a formal sit-down tasting with everyone tasting at the same time in a prescribed order, or a more casual affair, at which guests can serve themselves from a buffet-style table.

Allow 1–2 teaspoons of each honey per person. That amount will give everyone a good portion to taste. Present each honey in a small glass or white bowl so guests can see the color of each. Label each honey by floral source, so it's easily identified. Feel free to add additional information to the label about the region in which the honey was produced or about the beekeeper or apiary. It is not necessary

to display the honey's original bottle or jar. In fact, it's preferable not to, so as not to influence the tasters' opinions in any way. If you would like to include the original container, because it has an interesting design or label, place it behind that honey's sampling bowl. If there is no indication of the floral source, try to determine the floral source by using your senses and the information in chapter 3. You might consider printing a map and pinpointing each honey by location of origin for guests to see.

You can pick up small plastic tasting spoons at a local party supply warehouse or online. Make sure you provide a few clearly marked bowls around the table for used spoons. Provide napkins in several locations so guests can wipe their sticky fingers.

Serve sliced crusty bread and plain crackers in separate bowls around the table. Glasses and a pitcher of room-temperature water are essential so guests can cleanse their palates between honeys. Cheese, breads, nuts, fresh and dried fruits are all perfect accompaniments and should be served on a separate tray.

Prepare one copy of our Honey Color Chart and Honey Aroma and Tasting Wheel for each guest to refer to, as well as a Honey Tasting Scorecard for each guest, so they can make notes on what they've tasted. Don't forget to include pencils. Encourage conversation about the sensory qualities discovered in each honey. Enjoy, appreciate, and learn.

HONEY-TASTING ESSENTIALS:

- 4-6 different types of honey
- transparent glasses or white cups, preferably bowl shaped
- teaspoons, enough for each guest to taste each honey, plus some extra
- The Honey Connoisseur Color Charts
- The Honey Connoisseur Aroma and Tasting Wheels
- The Honey Connoisseur Tasting Scorecards, pencils
- water, at room temperature
- freshly-sliced green apple or plain bread
- napkins
- drinking glasses
- accompaniments

Honey Tasting Flights

Here are some suggestions for simple honey menus to serve at your honey tasting party:

SEASONAL

Spring menu: black locust, mesquite, orange blossom, tupelo; guajillo, linden, tulip poplar, inkberry, apple blossom

Summer menu: blueberry blossom, prickly pear, star thistle, tamarisk, kudzu; sourwood, clover, cranberry, cotton, buckwheat, avocado

Autumn menu: goldenrod, fireweed, spotted knapweed, purple loosestrife; saw palmetto, Japanese knotweed

REGIONAL

New England: blueberry, goldenrod, cranberry, buckwheat

Southeast: gallberry, tupelo, orange blossom, saw palmetto, kudzu

Pacific Coast: sage, star thistle, avocado, orange

Southwest: mesquite, catsclaw, guajillo, prickly pear, tamarisk

Northwest: fireweed, blackberry, apple blossom

Creating an Aroma Sensory Table

A great way to become acquainted with the aromas and flavors you will be experiencing while tasting honey is to create an aroma sensory table. A sensory table displays items from everyday life whose aromas correlate to flavors you'll likely experience in your honey. Ask guests to visit the table before the tasting and smell each item in order to experience and memorize its aroma. This is a great activity to do with friends, and it gets everyone to warm up and focus their olfactory senses.

Create the table by referring to the honey tasting wheel. Choose one item that represents one of the nine families in the center of the wheel. It is not necessary to represent every single item on the wheel for this experiment. Each time you create a sensory table you can change the items. If possible, include beeswax, bee pollen, and maybe even propolis, as they are essential to the honey tasting experience. You can either label each item by its family or try to identify which family each item falls into based on its aroma.

A few suggestions for your sensory table, by aroma family, follow:

Floral: roses, honeysuckle, or violets

Fruit: crispy apples, grapes, berries, or orange peel

Warm: chocolate, caramel, beeswax, crushed nuts, or marshmallows

Animal: leather, blue cheese, or daisies

Woody: fresh-cut wood, turpentine, cinnamon, or peppercorns

Fresh: anise seed, lavender, or peppermint

Chemical: plastic spoons, wet cardboard, or cabbage, soap

Spoiled: white vinegar, yeasty bread, ashes, or tobacco

Vegetal: fresh-cut grass, dried hay, green bananas or black tea leaves

How to Select and Purchase Good-Quality Honey

How can you decide whether a jar of honey is of good quality if you can't taste it before you purchase it? As a consumer, you have only the information on the label to guide you. Words like *natural, choice, fancy,* and *pure* may sound promising, but because they are not backed up by any government standards, they are not a reliable way to appraise the integrity of a honey. Also, clever marketing and attractive packaging can easily deceive the casual consumer into believing a honey is uncompromised. The following paragraphs present a few clues to help you evaluate a honey or at least give you a fairly accurate snapshot of what might be inside the jar.

FINDING A SOURCE

When it comes to choosing and purchasing honey, we recommend that you buy directly from your local beekeeper or farmer's market. Ideally, it's best to purchase honey closest to its source and from a beekeeper or producer who is happy to answer your questions. Ask them where the honey was produced, when and how it was harvested, and what season or floral source it was produced from. You will be surprised at how much information you can gather, and the beekeeper will also usually let you have a taste. If the person selling the honey is not capable of answering basic questions about the product, you might want to consider another source. When you find a source that you trust and enjoy, build a relationship with that beekeeper or producer and continue to expand your knowledge about honey.

PLASTIC OR GLASS?

The familiar squeeze bear honey bottle has been a symbol of honey for decades. It certainly is convenient and keeps sticky messes to a minimum. Now that you have experienced the delicate aromas and flavors of honeys, however, does a plastic bottle seem like the best way to preserve them? Plastic is associated with health risks and toxins. When it is exposed to high temperatures, those toxins can leak into the food stored inside. Glass repels food odors and residual flavors. Honey, like most foods just tastes fresher and cleaner when stored in glass. Look for a tight-fitting lid that seals well and, preferably, is of a high-quality metal that will not leave an unpleasant metallic taste on your fingers and mouth.

LABELING

It is advisable to purchase a jar that carries a basic label. Not only does the label indicate that the producer is a legitimate business, in the best scenario, it also conveys a sense of pride. The label should carry enough information about the product to allow you to make an informed purchase. Ideally, it should name the floral source, the location, and the producer. Most important, if the apiary's or beekeeper's name is not listed on the label, beware. Larger companies that import, pack, or trade honey do not reveal the name of the individual beekeeper or the location of the hives from which the honey was harvested. Only the distribution company's name is usually listed. Even if a honey label carries all of this important information, it does not guarantee a quality product or one that you will like.

Evaluating the Honey

Is it possible to choose a good-quality honey by simply observing what is inside the jar? When the beekeeper is not available, you may only have your own good judgment to rely on. Use what you have learned here to evaluate the visual qualities of honey you might purchase in a store. First, observe the color of the honey and make a few general observations and comparisons. We suggest comparing all of the store's honeys to each other, then, if possible, comparing them to other producers' honeys with similar floral sources. There should be variations between the colors of all of them, even the honeys from similar floral sources bottled by different producers. Note which honeys are transparent and which are cloudy. The honey that is cloudy rather than perfectly transparent is most likely the better choice. Look for signs of crystallization at the bottom of the jar. Although crystallization begins at the surface, where dust and pollen first collect, when sugar crystals form, they sink to the bottom of the jar where they are visible. Heavily crystallized honey will have most of the sugar pulled out of the solution and fermentation can become an issue. To avoid crystallization at home, honey should be stored at room temperature, not in a cool cupboard or in the refrigerator.

Take note of the conditions in which the honey is displayed. Is the temperature of the shop very cold or hot? Dramatic fluctuations in temperature may compromise honey or will cause early crystallization. It's never a good idea to purchase honey that has been sitting in a hot store window, especially if the honey is stored in plastic. Finally, observe the overall presentation of the honey and the containers. Scratched, dented, sticky, or dusty honey jars with labels that are peeling should not win your confidence regarding the quality of the product. Presentation counts.

PRICE

They say you get what you pay for, but that may not always be the case. Beekeepers selling their own honey generally set their honey prices at market value. Although those prices are often slightly higher than those of commercial producers, the amount of labor that goes into producing artisanal honey is rarely reflected in them. There's big difference in quality, however, and bee-keepers must work harder to educate their customers as to the unique characteristics of their honey. Honeys produced locally and seasonally in limited-harvest, or desirable single-source varietals like manuka, tupelo, or sourwood have name recognition, so expect to pay a bit more for them.

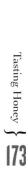

CHAPTER 6

PAIRING HONEY WITH CHEESE AND FOOD

As we have discovered, there is much more to honey than a sweet taste. Every honey has its own, unique flavor profile, bursting with the characteristics of its terroir. While it may be perfectly fine to dissolve a great honey in a cup of tea, its flavor has many other gifts to offer. When we pair an exquisite honey with the right cheese, the two flavors complement one another, creating a whole new level of flavor, in much the same way that pairing wine with cheese, meat, or any other dish brings out the flavor of both the wine and the food.

The secret to pairing these sweet and savory combinations lies in exploring the wide varieties of flavors and textures and then coming up with a combination that is balanced and pleasing to your palate. It's easy to recognize when you have created a harmonious pairing. Think about the taste equation of one plus one equals three in your mouth—meaning that the combination of that particular cheese and that honey will create a synergy of flavors that is far grander than the flavors of the individual parts. If one flavor dominates the other or covers it considerably, we might not consider the pairing balanced.

Pairing Honey and Cheese

Cheese is the perfect complement to honey, and you will quickly discover that there are countless pairings to please every palate. Our pairings do not require anything more than simply drizzling the honey over the cheeses.

Creating memorable honey and cheese pairings is an adventure not only in flavor but also in travel and culture. Cheese and honey are both terroir-driven agricultural products that reflect the region in which they were produced. Every cheese has a story, just as every honey does. The flavor profiles of cheeses are as diverse as those of honey and can be described as sweet, savory, earthy, grassy, musty, and floral. These flavors are dependent on the type of animal and its milk; the animal's regional diet; the season in which the cheese is produced; and the producer's flavoring agents, such as herbs, spices, or wood. Generally, cow's milk cheeses have a buttery richness, goat's milk has a tang, and sheep's is known for its mellow nuttiness. These qualities may vary depending upon the terroir of the cheese, so always taste before pairing.

Begin by picking out a few different cheeses at your local cheese shop or grocer. Ask the cheese monger for some suggestions; he or she will most likely offer you samples for tasting. Tasting cheeses is similar to tasting honey. Use your senses to identify flavors like grass, earth, or nuttiness. There are hundreds of flavors you might taste in cheeses. Cheese can be soft, runny, semi-soft, semi-hard, or hard; and those qualities will change as a cheese ages. Remember that texture and mouth feel are part of the overall tasting and pairing experience.

Once you choose your cheese, think about the flavors of honey and experiment with pairings to decide which ones you think would taste well together. When in doubt, choose cheeses and honeys that were harvested and produced in the same region, as they will reflect a mutual terroir.

- -

SOME SUGGESTIONS FOR CHEESES THAT PAIR WELL WITH HONEY,
and their tasting notes, follow to get you started:

- -

ASIAGO: Italian, cow's milk, rich, nutty yet mild, similar to Parmesan

CAMEMBERT: French, cow's milk, smooth, salty; runny texture

GORGONZOLA: Italian, cow's milk, rich, creamy, pungent; a stinky blue-veined cheese; soft texture

MANCHEGO: Spanish, sheep's milk, caramel flavors, salty and nutty; firm texture

MASCARPONE: Italian, cow's cream, buttery creamlike flavor; creamy texture

PECORINO ROMANO: Italian, sheep's milk, oily, granular, and salty; semi-hard

GARROTXA (ga-ROCH-ah): Spanish, goat's milk, milky and nutty; semi-soft

STILTON: English, cow's milk, punchy, strong smelling, and spicy

Different cheeses by type follow:

RIPE, PUNGENT, ACIDIC, AND AGGRESSIVE: aged cheddar, Comte, goat Gouda

SOFT: Brillat-Savarin, Camembert, and Robiola Rochetta

FIRM AND SALTY: Parmigiano-Reggiano, Manchego, Mimolette

BLUE CHEESE: Gorgonzola, Valdeon, Stilton

Basic Cheese & Honey Pairings

A soft, spreadable goat cheese pairs nicely with just about every honey because it has a mild creamy texture that enhances the flavors of the honey. The strong, musty flavors and crumbly texture of Gorgonzola pairs well with a rich, robust buckwheat, avocado or tamarisk honey because they are complex in flavors and make a bold statement. Try an earthy Brie cheese paired with a grassy alfalfa honey or a salty, nutty cheddar cheese paired with a tart, delicate apple honey. A fruity, smooth-textured blueberry honey with creamy ricotta is simply divine. Honeycomb with a triple cream is a sophisticated experience in textures.

Accompaniments

Adding accompaniments to the pairings you enjoy provides a whole new dimension to the tasting experience. Whether it is the crunchy texture of nuts, the tartness of dried cherries, or the crispiness and juiciness of a freshly sliced pear, you'll engage more of your senses while enjoying the multiple layers of flavors. Try introducing some of the foods from the list below to your cheese and honey pairings:

DRIED FRUITS
apricots, dates, cranberries, or cherries

NUTS
Marcona almonds, walnuts, pecans, or pistachios

FRESH FRUITS
fresh figs, berries, peaches, pears, or grapes

VEGETABLES
zucchini, olives, edamame, or sundried tomatoes

BREADS
crusty bread, ginger snaps, water crackers, pepper crackers, or herbal flatbreads

HERBS AND SPICES
fresh mint, cinnamon, nutmeg, ginger, or black pepper

Tasting Flights }

10 Perfect Honey and Cheese Pairings with Accompaniments

	HONEY	CHEESE	ACCOMPANIMENT
DARK AND DAZZLING	buckwheat—deep, malty, and chocolate flavors	Bayley's blue, Stilton, or Berkshire blue—bold, moldy flavors	fresh figs and tawny port
SWEET AND CREAMY	blueberry blossom—smooth, fruity	Ricotta—creamy, lemony notes or creamy Pierre Robert	toasted pine nuts
SWEET AND TOOTHSOME	fireweed—warm, caramel flavors	Pecorino Balze Volteranne—firm, nutty, green flavors	freshly sliced pears and pecans
EARTH AND GRASS	alfalfa—pleasant grass and stem flavors	Casatica di Bufala, Limburger, Nevat—buttery earthy goatiness	grilled peaches
HEAVEN ON EARTH	honeycomb	Délice de Bourgnone, Robiola Rocchetta, crottin—decadent creaminess	Marcona almonds, sauvignon blanc, Prosecco
FLOWERS AND FRUIT	tulip poplar—dark, rich flavors of raisins and prunes	La Perla or Ossau Iraty Vielle—smooth, buttery, nutty	strawberries with Banyan, a chocolate-flavored dessert wine
LEATHER AND LACE	chestnut—earthy and woody flavors	Ricotta di Capra goat cheese	prosciutto and figs
SMOKY AND SMOOTH	goldenrod—bright and floral	Nevat, Ossau Iraty Vielle, Piave—salty, nutty	dried cherries and chardonnay
BUTTER AND GRASS	Linden—green grassy flavors of apricot	Tomme Vaudoise—buttery, grassy flavors	green melon, fresh mint

Pairing honey with cheese and food }

179

Pairing Honey with Olive Oil or Balsamic

Extra virgin olive oils and balsamic vinegars have flavor notes as diverse as those of honey. Olive oil is made by grinding whole olives to extract the oils. Balsamic is made from a reduction of grapes. Both ancient foods complement honey in a wide range of recipes, including salad dressings, marinades, and glazes. Honey and olive oil or balsamic can be drizzled together over cheeses, chocolate, or fruit.

Simple Honey Tasting Platter

An easy and elegant way to incorporate honey into a dinner party is to create a honey tasting board that replaces an appetizer or dessert course.

When planning your menu, spend some time seeking out interesting, unusual, or rare honeys and the foods you'll enjoy pairing with them. Plan on 2–3 ounces of cheese per person. Include different textures; a few soft, semi-soft, and firm make a good balance to enhance the visual and tasting experience. Brie, goat, Camembert, blue, and Pecorino are good basic cheeses. Slice the cheese into wedges

or medallions and arrange them on a large dish or platter. Select accompaniments and place them either directly on the platter with the cheese or in a side dish. For optimum flavors, serve your honey and cheeses at room temperature.

Drizzle some honey over the cheeses and set some extra in small cups with spoons for additional sweetness; slice up some crusty breads and put them, along with water crackers or flatbreads, in baskets near the cheese platter. Serve wine, beer, or your favorite beverage to complete the experience. One white and one red wine work nicely, but you can add a sparkling wine like Champagne, Cava, or Prosecco, which pairs well with triple cream cheeses. Remind your guests not to double dip into the honeys, as water or food particles are not only unpleasant but will cause the honey to ferment prematurely. Designate a separate serving utensil for each honey and a separate knife for each cheese; hard cheeses require a sharp knife, and softer cheeses can be spread with a butter knife. Let the party begin!

Tasting Flights }

beyond Honey and
Cheese Pairings

Although cheese pairs perfectly with honey, there are many other types of foods and flavors that, when paired with honey, create heavenly taste sensations. Here are a few:

BUCKWHEAT HONEY
+
DARK CHOCOLATE

Why it works: Buckwheat has deep rich notes of chocolate and cherries that pair perfectly with dark chocolate.

LINDEN HONEY
+
CRISPY, GREEN MELON

Why it works: Linden honey has unripened, green notes that complement the tartness of a green melon.

GOLDENROD HONEY
+
SUNFLOWER BUTTER

Why it works: Goldenrod honey has intense floral notes that work well with the umami of all nut butters.

TULIP POPLAR HONEY
+
SOUR RED CHERRIES

Why it works: Tulip poplar honey has rich floral and dried fruit notes that complement tart cherries.

AVOCADO HONEY
+
VANILLA ICE CREAM

Why it works: Avocado's dark earthy flavors complement sweet, smooth vanilla cream.

TAMARISK HONEY
+
CRISPY BACON

Why it works: Tamarisk honey's rich, full body and smoky flavors complement the smoky fats of fried bacon.

FIREWEED HONEY
+
SLICED PEARS

Why it works: Fireweed's sweet notes of vanilla and fruit complement freshly the crisp taste of sliced pears.

SOURWOOD HONEY
+
GINGERBREAD COOKIES

Why it works: Sourwood honey has spicy notes of anise and cinnamon that pair well with spicy gingerbread.

ALFALFA HONEY
+
CORNBREAD

Why it works: Alfalfa honey has notes of dry hay that pair well with the earthy taste of corn.

ORANGE BLOSSOM HONEY
+
FRESH PINEAPPLE

Why it works: Orange blossom's full floral bouquet complements the fruity tart pineapple taste.

Simple Honey Drizzles

This section provides some easy ideas for enhancing everyday condiments with honey. These are perfect for spicing up your daily meals using ingredients you already have in your cupboard. Simply whisk together each ingredient with honey in a medium bowl to taste. Prepare to delight your taste buds:

Honey and olive oil — Pairs well with green and fruit salads.

Honey and balsamic vinegar — Pairs well with sliced fresh strawberries.

Honey and cocoa — Pairs well with vanilla ice cream.

Honey and mustard — Pairs well with fried chicken.

Honey and barbecue sauce — Pairs well with ribs and burgers.

Honey and soy sauce — Pairs well with sushi or grilled salmon.

Honey and sunflower or peanut butter — Pairs well with warm bread.

Honey butter with fresh garden sage — Melt the honey butter in a small saucepan over medium heat. Add fresh sage leaves, or your favorite garden herb, and sauté for 2 minutes until you smell the sage. Drizzle immediately over pasta or fish.

Burnt honey sauce — Burnt honey (miele cotta) is a delicacy in Italy and around the world and is used to deepen the flavors of many types of dishes. It's very easy to make — just be careful not to scorch it: In a small skillet, bring honey to a boil, then immediately reduce the heat and cook for 1 more minute. Drizzle over custard or panna cotta ("cooked cream"), over ice cream, or even ham or pasta.

Infusing Honey

Improving on nature's goodness can be difficult when it comes to pure honey.

However, strategically infusing honey with aromatic herbs, spices, or fruits can yield an added dimension of flavor. Herbs have health benefits, and infusing them in honey can be a delicious way to sooth a scratchy throat or a cold. Add infused honeys to tea or take them straight on a spoon. Spice- and fruit-infused honeys make great dressings, marinades, and glazes.

Infused honey is easy to make and takes very little time. The longer you let your infused honey sit before using it, the richer the flavor becomes. To begin, rinse the ingredients you will be using and dry them thoroughly before adding them to the honey. It is essential that the ingredients added are completely dry since excess water in and on freshly picked herbs or fruits could cause your honey to prematurely ferment. The drying process could take as long as twenty-four hours.

Once all the ingredients are dry, chop them fine and add them to the honey. Chopping the ingredients ensures the maximum flavor in the shortest time; however, you can add your ingredients whole if you'd prefer that. Use 1 cup of honey to 2 tablespoons of ingredient or to your taste.

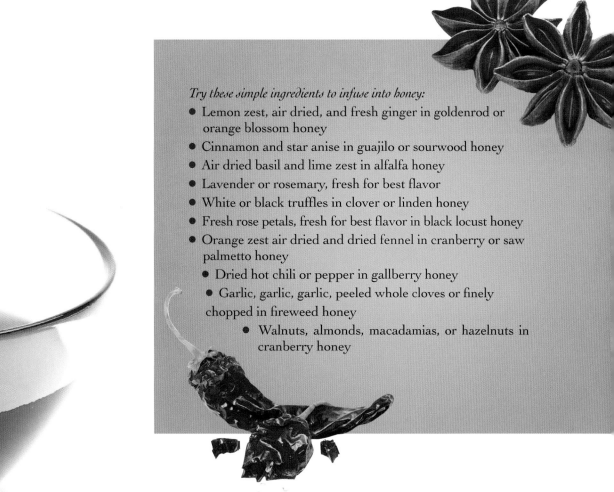

Try these simple ingredients to infuse into honey:

- Lemon zest, air dried, and fresh ginger in goldenrod or orange blossom honey
- Cinnamon and star anise in guajilo or sourwood honey
- Air dried basil and lime zest in alfalfa honey
- Lavender or rosemary, fresh for best flavor
- White or black truffles in clover or linden honey
- Fresh rose petals, fresh for best flavor in black locust honey
- Orange zest air dried and dried fennel in cranberry or saw palmetto honey
- Dried hot chili or pepper in gallberry honey
- Garlic, garlic, garlic, peeled whole cloves or finely chopped in fireweed honey
- Walnuts, almonds, macadamias, or hazelnuts in cranberry honey

Tomato, Peach, Basil and Summer Honey Salad

2 large, ripe peaches
2 large tomatoes
¼ cup balsamic vinegar
2 teaspoons gallberry or star thistle honey
2 cloves garlic, chopped
½ cup olive oil
1 teaspoon Dijon mustard
Fresh garden basil, shredded

Dice the peaches and tomatoes into bite-size pieces. Toss into a large bowl. Put all the remaining ingredients, for the dressing, into a separate medium bowl and mix well. Add the dressing to the tomatoes and peaches and toss until covered. Serve at room temperature.

Peanut Butter, Honey and Arugula Sandwich

Spread peanut butter and honey on your favorite slices of bread to taste. Garnish with fresh arugula leaves.

Honey Oat and Nut Energy Bars

SERVINGS: 8-10
PREP TIME: 25 minutes

½ cup peanut butter
1 cup honey
½ cup oatmeal
¼ cup sunflower seeds
¼ cup raisins
1 teaspoon flax seeds

In a small saucepan, mix peanut butter and honey over low heat until well blended, about 3 minutes. Remove from heat and add the oatmeal, sunflower seeds, raisins, and flax seeds until blended well. Scoop and spread about ½ thick on a flat baking sheet. Refrigerate for 30 minutes. Slice into triangles before serving.

Honey Figs with Goat Cheese and Pecans

SERVINGS: 6

Prep time: 25 minutes
1 cup finely chopped pecans
Coarse salt and freshly ground pepper
6-oz. log of goat cheese
12 fresh figs, Calimyrna or
    black mission, halved
Honey

Place the pecans in a shallow dish. Season
with salt and pepper. Roll the goat cheese
log in the pecans to evenly coat. Refrigerate
log until firm, then cut evenly into rounds.
Divide figs evenly between six dessert
plates. Top each fig half with a round of
pecan-crusted goat cheese. Drizzle 2
tablespoons of honey over each serving.
Serve immediately.

Honey Struck Chocolate Truffles

SERVINGS: 4   PREP TIME: 20 minutes

2 cups almonds, cashews, or walnuts
¾ cup cacao powder
5 dates, dried and pitted
¼ cup buckwheat honey
1 tablespoon coconut butter
Pinch of sea salt
Water, 2 tablespoons as needed
Shredded unsweetened coconut

In a food processor, grind the nuts of your choice. Add the cacao powder, dates, honey, coconut butter, and sea salt and blend. Add enough water to make the mixture moist but not wet. Hand-roll the honey-chocolate mixture into small balls, the size of cherries. Roll the truffles in the shredded coconut and store in the fridge for 1 hour before serving.

A

acidity: Pertaining to the level of sourness or tartness of flavor.

adult honey bee: The honey bee most people are familiar with. She flies, collects nectar and pollen, cares for the young, and can sting.

African honey bees: Several races of honey bees originating in Africa that have retained their ferocious behaviors in defense of their nests, food, and young.

aftertaste: See finish.

American Apicultural Areas (AAA): Distinct terroir regions in the United States where specific honey plants grow.

American foulbrood: A spore-forming bacterial disease infecting larvae honey bees that is controlled by antibiotics administered by beekeepers, or by the destruction through burning of the infected bees and the equipment they inhabited.

animal: Aroma or flavor family reminiscent of sweat, leather, or daisies.

Ark of Taste: An international list of foods threatened by industrial agriculture, environmental degradation, and homogenization. Part of the grassroots nonprofit organization, Slow Food, which is defending good, clean, and fair food.

artisanal honey: Honeys harvested by skilled beekeepers in limited quanties, using traditional methods, that have some common theme, but are not pure varietal or single source; for instance, spring honeys, summer honeys, and honeys from a particular location would all be artisanal honeys.

astringent: A honey that has a mouth feel of rough or dry, similar to the mouth feel of red wine or green and black teas.

B

balanced: Having a harmonious flavor profile.

beeswax: Technically, beeswax is a long chain fatty acid, composed simply of carbon, hydrogen, oxygen, and a few mineral compounds. Honey bees consume honey and special glands in their abdomens rearrange these molecules into a liquid, waxen-like product. This is expelled from the honey bee's body through the gland openings and hardens when it hits the cooler air outside of the bee's body. Beeswax is used to construct honeycomb to store honey in, to raise the young, and to provide a framework for the hive itself.

bitter: One of the five basic taste impressions; examples include grapefruit, greens, and coffee.

blended honey: Beekeepers can combine all the honeys their bees produced during the entire season and produce a single blend. Or, cheap tasteless honey can be blended with an expensive flavorful honey to produce a less expensive, less flavorful product. Or, sugar substitutes such as high fructose corn syrup, rice syrup, or even plain sugar can be added to honey to dilute its honey content and reduce the value.

bouquet: The total profile of an aroma.

bright: Having a flavor profile that is clean and clear to identify.

burnt: Flavor characteristic associated with the aroma of caramel or toasted notes.

buttery: Having a texture or flavor reminiscent of smooth butter.

C

camphorous: Having a flavor profile reminiscent of menthol or balsamic.

Carniolan bees: A race of bees that immigrated from the Italian peninsula to eastern European mountains. Springs are early and fast and these bees build populations rapidly in the spring and swarm early. However, they are also frugal and slow or stop brood production when resources are low to preserve their stores for leaner times.

chemical: Aroma or flavor family reminiscent of solvent or industrial chemicals.

chunk honey: A jar of honey containing a piece of comb honey surrounded by liquid honey.

citrus: Pertaining to the flavor family that includes fruits like orange, lemon, lime, tangerine, and grapefruit.

comb honey: Honey that is just as the bees made it and stored it in the hive. The beekeeper removes the wax honeycomb containing the honey still covered with the wax cappings the bees applied, package it, and sell it as is. It is the most natural form of honey there is.

complex: A perception of being multilayered in terms of flavors and aromas.

COOL: Country Of Origin Label; a law under Title X of the Farm Security and Rural Investment Act of 2002 that requires retailers to provide the country of origin on the label. The goal of this law is for consumers to see where their food is coming from. It is essentially ignored by many food producers, honey importers often included.

creamed honey: Honey allowed to crystallize under controlled conditions of temperature and crystal size, added by the beekeeper.

creamy: Fine particles and viscosity of a honey that gives an impression of a smooth texture.

D

deep: A flavor profile that has rich layers of flavors.

delicate: A flavor that is subtle, light, and pleasant.

drones: Male honey bees. At the height of the season, the largest population of drones is in the hive, which may reach 750 to 1000. During poor weather, winter, or times of stress, the colony quits raising drones, may remove and destroy drone larvae or pupae, and even remove and kill adult drones.

dry: A flavor profile reminiscent of straw, hay, or tea.

E

egg: The first stage in complete metamorphosis. Honey bee eggs take about three days to turn into the next stage, the larvae.

European bees: Any of many races of bees that developed in the European continent that had originally migrated north from Africa, but migrated to extremes in environment and evolved behaviors and biologies to survive winters, droughts, and the like.

extracting: Honey bees store honey in the hexagonal-shaped cells they make of beeswax, secreted from glands in their abdomens. When the cells are full of honey that's cured, they cover the cell with a thin layer of beeswax to protect it. These beeswax cells are contained in a rectangular wooden or plastic frame about an inch thick with cells of honey on both sides. To remove the honey, beekeepers place frames in an extracting machine, much like a lettuce spinner, spin the frames, and the honey moves out of the frames by centripetal force, leaving empty but reusable cells and frames and liquid honey at the bottom of the extractor.

F

fermentation: yeast, sugar, and water combine to make vinegar, and then alcohol. When honey, which is mostly sugar, has too much water (more that 18%) and contacts any of the many, many natural yeasts in the environment, alcohol forms. If the right amount of each is used, the result is a pleasant wine called mead. If the wrong amounts are used, the result is disgusting.

finish: The perceived taste a honey leaves behind after it is swallowed.

flash heating: Rapidly raising the temperature of honey in the microfiltering process to about 120 degrees F to 140 degrees F so it passes through filters rapidly and easily.

flavor profile: The total character of a honey as expressed in reference to aroma, taste, texture, and flavor.

floral: Aroma or flavor family reminiscent of flowers or perfume.

foragers: Adult female honey bees who spend their time searching for and gathering nectar, pollen, water, and propolis.

fresh: Aroma or flavor family reminiscent of camphorous cool rain or herbs, peppermint, lavender, or anise.

fructose: One of the six-carbon sugars the twelve-carbon sugar sucrose is broken down into when honey is made from floral nectar.

fruit: Aroma or flavor family reminiscent of fruit.
full-bodied: Rich and intense flavors; impressions that feel heavy in the mouth.

G

geographic indications: Certification that a product has certain specific sensory qualities, is produced according to traditional methods, or enjoys a unique reputation based upon its geographic origin.

GMO crops: Plants that have had their genes modified to add agricultural characteristics such as resistance to disease, toxins to kill pests, or resistance to herbicides.

goût de terroir: Taste of earth.

green: Grassy, vegetal notes reminiscent of unripened fruit.

guard bees: Adult honey bees that tend to hive defense. They may be at the front door, near the queen, at the top entrance, or anywhere an intruder may gain access. They have reached the age in which their bodies produce the most venom, and they react the fastest when alarm pheromone is released in the hive by other guards.

H

herbaceous: Typical flavors reminiscent of the aromatic, vegetal leaves of green herbs.

HFCS: High fructose corn syrup, a fructose sugar derived from corn either by adding chemicals to make the sucrose molecule break or enzymes to do the same; either way, it is not a natural product.

hoarding: The instinct that honey bees and some other bees have to continue to collect and store food long after they have enough to survive the drought/cold/wet/dearth season when no outside source of food is available.

hydroscopic: The property of a material to absorb moisture from the air. Honey is hydroscopic, so a jar of honey left open will absorb air moisture.

I

invasive plants: Many honey plants in the United States originated in other countries. As such, they have few natural enemies or controls and often grow unchallenged. This is good for beekeepers, but very often these invaders crowd out native plants and the wildlife that depends on them in a given area. They are definitely a mixed blessing.

Italian bees: A race of bees that immigrated from Africa to the Italian peninsula and adapted to the semitropical climate. They are known to be productive, gentle, and produce brood early and late in the season.

L

Langstroth, Reverend Lorenzo Lorraine: Known as the father of modern beekeeping. Developed the modern beehive with movable frames so beekeepers can easily manage their colonies and extract honey with minimal disturbance to the brood nest. Before the invention of the Langstroth hive, bees were kept in woven skeps or gum logs.

larva: The second stage of honey bee metamorphosis. This is similar to the caterpillar stage of butterflies and lasts different lengths of time for workers, drones, and queens.

local honey: How close is local? Some say the same county, some within 100 miles, and some even declare that within 400 miles is considered local. Ask where the honey was produced and decide for yourself.

log hives: The primary hive used by African beekeepers, it is simply a hollow log with the ends capped and hung in trees. Swarms move in, set up housekeeping until the dry season begins, and move on. Beekeepers harvest the remaining honey and rehang the hive.

M

microfiltered honey: Typical filtering technique for most commercial grade honey. Honey is flash heated to about 120 degrees F to 140 degrees F, forced through several filters to remove all particulate matter, wax flakes, dust, and pollen, and then flash cooled back to about 100 degrees F and bottled. This drives off some of the more volatile aromatics and certainly removes any particulate matter characteristics, but essentially leaves the honey unharmed.

mouth feel: A sensory attribute to a physical characteristic of food.

N

nectar: A liquid produced by plants that is rich in sugars and transported from the leaves where the sugar is formed to flowers. It is stored in nectaries or in extrafloral nectaries, often on the underside of leaves. Nectar, a rich carbohydrate, is the bribe flowers use to entice bees to visit and assist in pollination.

nurse bees: The youngest adult bees. For the first three to six days, their brood food glands are operating full bore and they tend to the young, the queen, and keep the house clean. Eventually, they age to become food handlers, guards, undertakers, and foragers.

P

palate: The range of an individual's ability to recognize flavors.

palate fatigue: Also known as collapsed palate, the point at which a person can no longer experience tastes or flavors.

petal: Almost always the show part of a flower that attracts pollinators. Sometimes it's not the petal but the sepal.

pistals: The female portion of the reproductive part of a plant, consisting of the pollen receptive area; the tube the pollen must traverse to reach the ovary so that union produces a seed.

pollen: The male portion of the reproductive process of plants, produced in the anthers, suspended above the flower by the stamens.

propolis: A resinous material honey bees gather from, primarily developing leaf buds, exuded by the buds to protect them from disease and insects. Bees gather this material, which can be many colors and contain differing proportions of a variety of materials, depending on the source. It has antimicrobial and antibacterial properties and bees use the substance to help sanitize their hives, to fill small spaces, and to smooth rough areas. It is soft and sticky in warm weather, but hard and brittle when it is cold. Beekeepers harvest this and process it for medicinal uses for humans.

pungent: Strong, spicy, hot, heady, sharp, biting.

pupa: The cocoon state of honey bee metamorphosis. When they reach this stage in their beeswax cell, they spin a thin cocoon and the cell is covered with a thin layer of beeswax by the house bees to protect the developing larvae, which in a few days emerge as adults.

Q

queen: The only sexually complete female in the hive. She mates with ten to twenty or more drones shortly after she emerges as an adult, then begins a life of egg laying, pheromone production, and being attended to with great care by the nurse bees in the hive. This continues until she ages past a productive point, is injured, runs out of sperm from all those matings, becomes too old to produce pheromones, or, because of its success, the hive becomes large enough to divide itself and cast a swarm. About half the bees in the hive leave to form a new home, accompanied by the old queen. The remaining bees, of course, immediately raise a new queen and their colony continues as before.

R

raw honey: There is really no legal definition for raw honey, but there are many sort-of definitions. Basically, raw honey is not heated above 105 degrees F (the temperature of a desert hive), is not filtered at all, but is often strained to remove disagreeable debris developed in the extracting process. And that's it. Not heated, not filtered. Raw.

refractometer: A simple machine that measures the percent of solids suspended in a liquid sample—the solids being sugars in the case of honey—thus a reading gives the moisture content (the remaining percent of the sample) of the product. Honey should contain less than 17.5% moisture to be stable.

Russian bees: A hybrid mix of several races of bees moved to the eastern portions of Russia as the Russians colonized that part of their country. They are partially Carniolan, Caucasian, Italian, German Black, and others. These were some of the first bees exposed to Varroa mites, so they have had the longest time to adapt and become resistant or tolerant of them in a hive. The U.S. Department of Agriculture imported several varieties and has been selecting those most resistant, productive, and gentle for U.S. beekeepers to use.

S

savory: One of the five basic tastes, also known as umami.

sensory evaluation: The process of tasting and using the senses to taste honey.

salty: One of the five basic tastes described as briny or brackish.

sour: One of the basic tastes, acid, lemon.

spicy: Food that has a piquant, hot, fiery, burning taste; spiced, zesty, peppery.

spoiled: Aroma or flavor family reminiscent of fermentation, earthy, or yeasty.

sucrose: Common table sugar, and the most common sugar in floral nectar. When harvested by bees, an enzyme is added by the bees to break it into glucose and fructose sugars, which are digestible by bees and humans.

surplus: The amount of honey in excess of what the bees will need in times of dearth that is available to the beekeeper.

survivor: Any hybrid mix of honey bees that continues to thrive even when exposed to Varroa mites, extremes in weather, food shortages, and the like.

sweet: One of the five basic tastes, candied, sugary, saccharine.

T

tart: The perception of sour or acid on the taste buds, for example, lemon.

taste: The five taste impressions are sweet, sour, bitter, salty, and umami.

tasting notes: The sensory descriptions of honey.

terroir: The combination of characteristics of soil, location, and weather in any given region that affects honey plants, honey bees, and the honey harvest.

texture: The tactile quality of a honey as it feels in your mouth, also referred to as mouth feel.

thixotrophic: Honey that has a gel-like consistency until stirred, when it turns to liquid.

trans-shipping: Honey produced in one country, sent to a second country, fraudulently labeled as produced in the second country, and then exported to a third country to avoid tariffs or taxes.

U

umami: One of the five basic tastes, also known as savory.

uncapping: Removing the pure beeswax covering the cells filled with honey.

ultra-filtered honey: When honey is ultra-filtered, water is added to dilute the liquid, it is heated to near boiling, and then passed through ceramic filters with openings so small all proteins, pollen, particulate matter, some of the aroma, and larger sugar molecules and even some of the color molecules are removed. What remains is not honey, but rather a somewhat sweet syrup.

V

varietal honey: Often also called single source honey, it is honey collected from a hive by the beekeeper that was all collected from a single type of plant—orange blossoms only, for instance—a pure variety or single source.

vegetal: Aroma or flavor family reminiscent of green or dried grass or tea.

viscosity: Mouth feel, the body or weight of honey on your tongue.

W

warm: Aroma or flavor family reminiscent of burned, smoky, or nutty notes.

wild flower honey: A name often used when the beekeeper does not know the flowers the bees collected the honey from, blending in all manner of seasonal, artisanal, and even single source honeys in a single blend

woody: Aroma or flavor family reminiscent of wood bark or chips.

cotton, 49
Country of Original Label (COOL) law, 144
cow's milk cheeses, 176
cranberries, 74–75
cranberry honey, 49, 75, 161
Crane, Eva, 160
Crane, James, 160
CRP. *See* Conservation Reserve Program
crystallization, 15, 111, 121, 173
crystallized honey, 17–18, 154, 158–159
cut comb honey, 17
cutting honey, 137

dandelions, 50
darker honey
    composition of, 16
    minerals in, 27
    seasons for, 38
    tasting, 152, 157
Denominazione di Origine Protetta (DOP),
    44
Department of Agriculture, U.S., 147, 160
Department of Commerce, U.S., 143
Department of Homeland Security, U.S.,
    136, 141
desert honeys, 26, 90, 106–113, 158
disaccharides, 15
diseases of honey bees, 42, 141
DOP. *See* Denominazione di Origine
    Protetta
double dipping, 181
Drambuie, 117
drizzles, honey, 184
drones, 10, 21

earth. *See* terroir
Egypt, 9–10, 44
endangered honeys, 97, 106, 109
Energy Bars, Honey Oat and Nut, 190
enzymes, 11, 15–16, 18, 21
Europe, 43–44. *See also specific countries*
European Union, 43, 44, 128, 146
evaluating honey, 172–173
extracted honey (liquid honey), 17
extraction of honey, 12, 17, 138
extractor, 12

fermentation of honey, 15–16, 138, 154,
    157, 181, 185
Figs, Honey, with Goat Cheese and
    Pecans, 193
finish or end, 165
fireweed, 49, 76–77
fireweed honey, 77, 150, 158, 161, 179,
    183
flavor families, 163, 165
flavor notes, 163, 165

flavor of honey, 161, 163. *See also* pairing
    foods and honey; *specific* honey
    aroma and, 150–151, 159, 161, 163,
        171
    burned or chemical, 43
    distinguishing, 150
    impacts on, 43, 149
    smoky or burned, 157
    taste compared to flavor, 159, 161
flavor profiles
    of cheese, 176
    of honey, 16, 152
flowers
    flower fidelity, 15
    nectar guides on, 11
    pollination of, 12, 15
food. *See* pairing foods and honey
foods, adulterated, 136–137, 141
foraging honey bees, 10–11, 15, 37
forests, 49, 76–77
frames
    beeswax comb in, 17
    coaxing bees away from, 12, 43
    uncapping, 12
France
    honeys from, 44, 114, 118–119
    terroir and, 23, 43–44, 118–119
fructose, 15–16, 18, 161
fruits
    as accompaniment, 168, 178
    Tomato, Peach, Basil and Summer
        Honey Salad, 187
fume board, 12

gallberry, 78–79
gallberry honey, 78–79, 152
genetically modified organisms (GMOs),
    128–129, 144, 146–147
    pollen, 128, 146–147
Geographic Indications (GI), 43
glass or plastic containers, 172
Gleanings in Bee Culture, 79
glucose, 15–16, 18, 161
glucose oxidase, 16
GMOs. See genetically modified organisms
goat's milk cheeses, 176
    Honey Figs with Goat Cheese and
        Pecans, 193
goldenrod, 59, 80–82
goldenrod honey, 80, 81–82, 179, 182
Gonnet, Michel, 160
goût de terroir (taste of earth), 23
granulated honeys, 158–159. *See also*
    crystallization; crystallized honey
granulation, 111
grapefruit honey, 90
grayanotoxins, 130

Great Plains region, 33
Greece, 44, 126–127
guajillo, 109
guajillo honey, 106, 109

harvests. *See* honey harvests
health benefits
    of honey, 17
    of royal jelly, 21
heather, 116–117
heating honey, 16, 140, 156, 173
herbs and spices, 178. *See also specific*
    herbs
hives. *See* beehives
HMF. *See* hydroxymethylfurfural
hoarding instinct, 134
holly honey, 73
honey. *See also specific honeys and*
    countries
    acidity of, 16, 161
    anti-bacterial properties of, 16, 123,
        162
    blending, 137–138
    composition of, 15–16, 140, 161
    cutting, 137
    drizzles, 184
    evaluating, 172–173
    extraction of, 12, 17, 138
    fermentation of, 15–16, 138, 154, 157,
        181, 185
    health benefits of, 17
    heating, 16, 140, 156, 173
    infusing, 185
    kinds of, 16–17
    medical uses for, 10, 122–123
    minerals in, 16
    moisture in, 138, 140, 157
    names for, 26, 152
    origin of, 10, 16, 152
    pH of, 16
    presenting, 152, 168
    price of, 173
    quality of, 10, 16
    ripening process of, 15–16
    science and art of making, 10–11
    selecting and purchasing, 172
    storage of, 9–10, 16, 157
    uses for, 10, 17, 122–123
    varieties of, 10
    water in, 15, 138, 143, 173
    weight of, 157–158
Honey: A Comprehensive Survey (Crane,
    E.), 160
honey ambassadors, 160
honey and cheese pairings, 161, 175–176
    accompaniments for, 178–179
    basic, 177

Some References on Plants that Produce Honey

There are a handful of good books and resources that will give you all the information you are looking for about honey producing plants.

BOOKS

Louisiana Honey Plants, Dale Pollet, LSU Ag Center, LA Coop Extension Service

Plants For Beekeeping In Canada and the northern States, Jane Ramesy, IBRA

Weeds Of California and Other Western States, Vol. I & II, DiTomaso & Healy, CA Weed Science Society

Wetland Plants of Western Wasington and North-western Oregon, Sarah Cooke, Seattle Audubon Society

American Honey Plants, Frank Pellett, Dadant & Son (reprints available)

Weeds Of The Northeast, Richard H. Uva, Joseph C.Neal, Joseph M. DiTomaso, Comstock Publishing

Texas Honey Plants, Sanborn & Scholl, Dept. Of Ent., College Station, TX

Honey Plants Of California, M.C. Richter, CA

Experiment Station

Weeds Of The South, Bryson and DeFelice, Univ. GA Press

Silvics Of Forest Trees, H. A. Fowells, USDA Handbook 271

Honey Plants Of North America, John Lovell, A. I. Root Company (reprint available)

Insect Pollination Of Cultivated Crop Plants, S. E. McGregor, USDA Hand book 496 (reprint available)

The USDA Invasive Plant List
Invasive Plants list from various states, and the USDA Plants list.gov

THE INTERNET

There's certainly a wealth of information and misinformation on the Internet. How are you to know if the information you're accessing is accurate? We have a rule when using the Internet: The source needs to verify itself with scientific references, which themselves have to be easily verified. It's not a foolproof system, but it's proven to be a reliable system for us.

Start with Wikipedia. We advise you to start a search on this site when looking for plant information because the sources are plentiful and often most of what you need can be found there. Don't assume, however, that Wikipedia is perfect, because sometimes it's more opinion than fact. A good Wikipedia entry always lists the sources used to present the data.

Always reliable is the USDA plants database: plants.usda.gov

But always check further, usually with a University reference.

Of course you may want additional information on a particular plant. If you have succumbed to our descriptions of some of these varietal honeys, perhaps becoming a beekeeper is in your future and growing one of these plants to produce the honey is interesting. For instance, one avocado tree can provide much in the way of that honey for a hive in the back yard and garden forums can provide insights that sound science sometimes overlooks. A good site to look at is: forums.gardenweb.com, where personal experience can often outweigh hard science. So be sure to check out sources like those as well.

For more information on honey tasting visit www.americanhoneytastingsociety.com.